CU00765179

A Brief History of Cyprus, Second Edition

Copyright © 2020 by Tommy Clark

Cover by Nathan Holliday

All rights reserved. No part of this book may be reproduced or transmitted in any form or by any means without written permission from the author.

ISBN 978 1 5272 6852 4

DEDICATION

To my mum and sisters, so you can finally learn about Cyprus!

with thanks to Katie, Nora and Molly

CONTENTS

INTRODUCTION

Cyprus is a small island in the Eastern Mediterranean Sea. It measures 140 miles east to west and 60 miles north to south – just under half the size of Wales – and has a population of just a little over a million. Despite its small size the island has been an important strategic territory for many large world powers over the course of its history, which has had a great influence on the state of the island.

Cyprus today, is divided in to two. The Turkish Republic of Northern Cyprus covers roughly 35% of the island in the north, and the Republic of Cyprus around 60% in the south. The remaining 5% is split between UN-controlled buffer zones and British sovereign military bases.

The two countries on the island have very different relationships with the international community.

The Republic of Cyprus was given its independence in 1960 by the British, and has been a member of the UN since its inception. In 2004 it joined the European Union and, at the time of writing, has been a high income country according to the World Bank since 1988.[1] The economy is based mainly on tourism and financial services, and operates as an offshore tax haven to countries like Russia and Israel.[2]

In contrast, the TRNC declared its own independence unilaterally in 1983 and is recognised as a sovereign state only by Turkey. Pakistan and Bangladesh briefly recognized the state following its declaration, but withdrew their recognition after pressure from the United Nations.[3] Severe international embargoes are in place against TRNC[4] which prohibits their dealings with the Universal Post Union, the International Civil Aviation Organisation, and the International Air Transport Association. Their football teams can not compete in FIFA competitions, their food certificates were deemed unacceptable for the European Union in 1994, and they are not recognised by the World Trade Organisation. Because of these restrictions, all imports, exports and flights have to happen using Turkey as an intermediary.

---

[1] (World Bank, 2020)

[2] In recent years, the country's "aggressive tax planning" has drawn criticism from the EU's 'Special Committee on Financial Crimes, Tax Evasion and Tax Avoidance' which referred to Cyprus as displaying the "traits of a tax haven". (European Parliament, 2019)

[3] (UN Security Council Resolution 541 and 550, 1983, 1984)

[4] (Pegg, 1998, p. 117)

In 2004, the EU pledged that they were "determined to put an end to the isolation of the Turkish Cypriot community and to facilitate the reunification of Cyprus by encouraging the economic development of the Turkish Cypriot community"[1]. The European Parliament even discussed a proposal to trade directly with TRNC on 10th June 2010. Both times, the Greek Cypriots blocked any co-operation. The Greek Cypriot foreign minister at the time of the talks went so far as declaring that the southern Republic of Cyprus would "use all the institutional and political procedures we have at our disposal"[2] to block any EU trade with the Turkish Republic of Northern Cyprus.

The whole island was at one point the same country, where people from both the Turkish-speaking Muslim community and the Greek-speaking Orthodox community co-existed peacefully as neighbours.

So, what went wrong?

---

[1] (Commission of the European Communities, 2004)
[2] (Cyprus News Agency: News in English, 2010)

GEOGRAPHY AND ANCIENT HISTORY

Cyprus sits at the crossroads of Asia, Europe and North Africa, just 50 miles or so south of the coast of mainland Turkey, and around 500 miles east of Greece.

This location, at the meeting point of three continents, has been important throughout the islands history and has made it the subject of interest by world powers who have wanted to dominate trade, territory, or even ideology, across the continents and the Mediterranean.[1] Due partly to this, Cyprus has been conquered by many of the big empires throughout history.

Trade has always been important throughout the small island's history. In the Roman era, for example, the main supply of copper was mined on the island of Cyprus (copper is named after Cyprus: the word originates from the Latin word Cyprium or, literally, Cyprian metal)[2]. The Venetians, during their time in possession of Cyprus, used the island as a base to

---

[1] (Özkul, 2020)
[2] (Merriam-Webster Inc., 2020)

4

disrupt Ottoman trade with North Africa.[1] The island gained a renewed importance once again in the 19th Century when the French and British wished to trade with India and North Africa.[2] Even in the modern day, Cyprus is located on the busy shipping and air routes which link Western Europe to Africa and the East.

The island's location has also made it militarily important. Today, Britain maintains military bases on the Greek side of the island and has utilised those bases in recent years for UK and US led military operations and bombing campaigns in Syria, Afghanistan and Iraq. This wasn't the first time the Brits used the island in this way, having sent British jets from the island to bomb Egypt[3] during the Suez Crisis in the 1950s. The island was even used as a launching pad by the Crusaders for their attacks on the Muslim world, and for defence against the Mongol advance from Syria[4] as far back as the middle ages.

---

[1] (Geopolitical Futures, 2020)
[2] (Özveren, 2012)
[3] (The National, 2020)
[4] (Menache, 2003)

A timeline of the ancient empires

The first written historical source shows Cyprus under Assyrian rule. The Assyrian empire that ruled the island would have been the most powerful in the world at the time, with their homeland being based across parts of modern-day Iraq, Turkey, Iran and Syria. They employed advanced military tactics, many of the processes that future large empires would employ, and according to many historians were the first true empire in the world.[1]

> **627BC:** Cyprus gained independence from the Assyrians following the death of Ashurbanipal, the last great Assyrian king, and operated as independent city kingdoms ruled by the Cypriot kings.

> **570BC:** Cyprus was conquered by the Egyptians, who ruled the island briefly, and had a significant impact on ceramics and art on the island.[14]

---

[1] (Mark, 2014)
[2] (Hirschfeld, 2010)

525BC: The Persians took control. Under the Persians, the kings of Cyprus continued to rule without much interference but paid tribute to Persia. Cyprus also supplied armies and ships for Persia's foreign campaigns. In fact, in 480BC, Cyprus contributed 150 ships to the Persian military expedition to invade Greece.[15]

525BC – 333BC: Athenian Greeks tried unsuccessfully on numerous occasions to take Cyprus from the Persians. The Cypriots at the time were not interested in being ran by the Greeks however. According to E. Gjestard, "The Cypriot kings had no interest in exchanging Persian domination for an Athenian who would probably not respect their privileges as Persia did"[2].

333BC: Cyprus once again changed hands in battle. This time, being conquered by the Macedonian king, Alexander the Great.

323BC: After a very short period in power, at the age of 32, Alexander the Great died suddenly. His sudden death, without an obvious heir, led to the dissolution of his empire and the end of any aspirations that the Ancient Greek empire of Macedonia might one day dominate the world.

322BC – 312BC: Alexander the Great's empire was split up and fought over by his generals in a series of battles known as the 'Wars of Alexander's Successors'.

The main two claimants of Cyprus were Antigonus I Monophthalmus in Syria, and Ptolemy I Lagus in Egypt.

312BC: Ptolemy, one of Alexander the Great's field marshals[3], captured the island and Cyprus became a part of Ptolemaic Egypt.

58BC: The Roman Empire annexed Cyprus, but gifted it back to the last queen of Egypt – Cleopatra – to rule.

35BC: The island became a Roman province again shortly before Cleopatra's death, and stayed that way for the next 600 years or so.

[1] (Parker, 1976, pp. 30-38)
[2] (Gjerstadt, 1979, pp. 230-254)
[3] (M.Ellis, 1994, p. 1)

Roman Cyprus featured prominently in Roman trade in the Eastern Mediterranean during this time. As previously mentioned, copper was the islands main export, but Cyprus was also known for its olive oil – Strabo once said "in fertility Cyprus is not inferior to any one of the islands, for it produces both good wine and good oil"[1]. Olive oil containers from this time period have been found in Egypt, implying trade between the two countries, and evidence for trade in this period has also been found with Cilicia (now modern day Turkey) and Syria.[2]

The Roman empire then split into two. This split explains the culture, language and religion on the 'Greek' side of the island in the current day.

---

[1] (Papacostas, 2001, p. 112)
[2] (Papacostas, 2001, p. 153)

A HISTORICAL BACKGROUND

The Byzantine Empire

By the 3rd century AD, the Roman empire had become too vast to govern centrally from Rome, covering the land from Britain and mainland Europe all the way to Egypt and the Levant. The Roman emperor Diocletian decided at this point to appoint his fellow officer Maximian as co-emperor in 286AD.

The newly promoted co-emperor reigned in the Western Empire, which included central Europe, Italy and the British Isles. Diocletian himself reigned in the Eastern Empire, which included – amongst other places – Greece, Anatolia (modern day Turkey), Egypt, and of course, Cyprus.

Eastern and Western Romans at the time did not consider themselves independent of each other and referred to themselves on the whole as Romans. They thought of the split as nothing more than an administrative efficiency, but in practice they were actually ran almost entirely independently from one another. Although they would always refer to and identify themselves at the time simply as Romans, the Eastern Roman empire is referred to by modern day historians as the 'Byzantine Empire', named so after the name of the capital city of the Eastern half of the empire: Byzantium (modern day Istanbul)[1].

Whilst the western empire became Latin-speaking Roman Catholics, the Byzantines became Greek-speaking Orthodox Christians. The 'Greek' in 'Greek Orthodox' refers to the Byzantine empire which created the church, in the same way the 'Roman' in 'Roman Catholic' refers to the western Romans that created theirs. Today, you can still see Byzantine flags waving outside Greek Orthodox churches, including in Cyprus.

Arab-Byzantine condominium

Around 650AD, the Arabs believed that Byzantine Cyprus posed a threat to Arab positions on the Syrian coast and could be easily neutralised. They raided and quickly conquered the capital, but not the whole island.[2]

---

[1] (Brooks, 2006, p. 1)
[2] (Lynch, 2016, p. 539)

This raid is also notable for being the one in which a relative of the prophet Muhammad, Umm-Haram, fell from her mule and was killed near the Salt Lake at Larnaca. She was buried in that spot. Later, in Ottoman times, the Hala Sultan Tekke was built around her tomb and still stands there today.

In 688AD, the Byzantine emperor and the Arab caliph reached an unprecedented and novel agreement. The island was ran as an Arab-Byzantine "condominium" where tax revenues where shared by both powers. According to historian Zavagno, this sharing of power "bred a fertile terrain of political, economic and cultural ambiguity" [1], as Arab Muslims moved to the island to live alongside Orthodox Christians.

Despite the unusual situation, archaeological evidence indicates uninterrupted prosperity during the Arab-Byzantine period.[2]

Towards the end of 1st Century AD, the Byzantines reconquered the island for themselves, deporting many of the Muslim inhabitants of the island.

---

[1] (Zavagno, 2013, p. 20)
[2] (Lynch, 2016, pp. 541-542)

The Crusaders

On a crusade to conquer Jerusalem, Richard I – the King of England – was separated in a storm from his fiancée – the future queen of England – and his sister. When he arrived in Cyprus on 1st June 1191 to look for them, he found his future bride and sister shipwrecked and being held by the island's Byzantine ruler. The English King went on to conquer the entire island of Cyprus, holding the Byzantine emperor prisoner until his death a few years later.[1]

Richard I occupied Cyprus and raised taxes, encountering hostility from the local population. When the Cypriots believed their freedom might be at stake to the English invaders they staged a revolt. They were defeated, but the hostility made Richard I question whether the island was worth keeping, and, in need of money for his Christian crusades, he sold the island to the Knights Templar for 100,000 bezants.[2]

The Knights Templar were Christian crusaders who ruled their islands brutally, keeping Muslims they came across as slaves.[3] Their ruling style led to even greater opposition from the inhabitants of Cyprus.

---

[1] (Baldwin & Dickson, 2019)
[2] (Newman, 1940)
[3] (Finkel, 2012, p. 118)

Feeling unable to rule the island by force, they quickly gave it back to Richard I.

The English King soon after gifted the troublesome island to his friend, French knight Guy de Lusignan, in a successful attempt to placate him after he lost his crown as King of Jerusalem to Richard I's nephew. This started the almost 300 year reign over Cyprus by the French royal house of Lusignan.

The Mamluks

The de Lusignan family started to lose their grip of the island around the 15th Century. In 1426, the Cypriot king Janus lost the battle of Khirokitia, and the Kingdom of Cyprus were made to pay tribute to the Mamluk Sultanate.

The Mamluk Sultans were Turkish-speaking Sunni Muslims, referred to by Arabic sources at the time as 'The State of Turkey'.[1]

Venetian Cyprus

Cyprus, still ruled by the House of Lusignan, but now a tributary to the Mamluks, and with commercial

---

[1] (Yosef, 2013, pp. 7-34)

rights and other privileges already given to the Venetian merchants on the island, was starting to fade. The country allied itself to Venice to save itself from being dismembered.[1]

In 1468, Cyprus was linked to the Ventian noble family by marriage, before being sold officially to the Republic of Venice in 14 March 1489.

The Venetians ruled the island for the next 82 years, and aimed to profit from their acquisition, taking most of the money they made back to Venice.

Their reign was marked with harsh treatment of the locals, who were treated as personal property – "worse than slaves" according to one sixteenth century traveller.[2] Serfs were able to buy their freedom but taxes and obligations to the Venetian rulers were still harsh even for the free.[3] The poverty for the Cypriots were so extreme that many fled to Rhodes or to various parts of the Ottoman Empire.

The Venetian reign was also marked by almost constant fighting with the Ottomans, who had since annexed and defeated both the Turkish-speaking

---

[1] (Solsten, 1991, p. 16)
[2] (Oberling, 1982, p. 2)
[3] (Smilden, 2007)

16

Mamluk Sultanate (for which Cyprus was still paying tribute) in 1517, and the Byzantine Empire (from which most of the Greek-speaking Orthodox inhabitants of Cyprus had descended) in 1453.

THE OTTOMANS AND THE BRITISH

The Ottomans take Cyprus

Cyprus – surrounded on all sides by Ottoman territory, and a tributary state of the now-Ottoman Mamluks – was always going to be an interesting prospect for the Ottoman Empire. On top of that, the Venetians had decided to provide protection to pirates who plagued trade between the Ottoman heartland of Anatolia (modern day Turkey) and Ottoman Egypt. This was the final straw for the Sultan Selim II, who vowed to conquer Cyprus. The Sultan gained a favourable judicial opinion to invade, based on the justification that Cyprus was a 'former land of Islam'.[1]

The Ottomans also held the sympathies of the Cypriot population[2] (who were mostly Byzantine descended Greek Orthodox people, and therefore slaves under Venetian rule). There are reports of Greek-speaking Cypriots travelling to Istanbul to ask for Turkish help against the Venetians, as well as of a

---

[1] (Finkel, 2012, p. 158)
[2] (Goffman, 2002, pp. 156-157)

delegation of Cypriot serfs in 1569 who petitioned the Grand Vizir Mehmet Sokolli for Turkey to occupy Cyprus.[1]

In early 1570, both the Venetians and the Ottomans knew that war was imminent, and so the Venetians attempted to find allies. They eventually aligned themselves with the Holy League – an alliance of Catholic states, arranged by the pope, that had been organised to fight the Muslim Ottoman empire – but it was too late and the Ottoman empire took Nicosia on September 9, 1570. The Republic of Venice eventually lost the war and signed a treaty with the Ottomans whereby Cyprus became an Ottoman province and the Venetians paid them 300,000 ducats (the Venetian currency of the time).

Life under the Ottoman Empire

After hundreds of years of oppressive rule for the Cypriots, life under the Ottomans was very different.

The Venetians had sold and owned the local Byzantine-descended Greek Orthodox population as slaves, whereas the Ottomans banned serfdom when they came to power. Cypriots were finally given back

---

[1] (Smilden, 2007)

their freedom, were allowed to own their own property, and were able to transfer ownership to others by way of inheritance, gifts or sale – something they had not been allowed to do under the Venetians.

As in most of the Ottoman empire, the Turkish rulers were much more interested in securing tax incomes than in the religious conversion of their countries, and so the local population, including the Greek Orthodox Cypriots, also gained back their freedom to practice the Greek and Byzantine religion and culture. Religious locals were given more freedom under the Ottomans than they would have gotten anywhere else in Europe at the time.[1]

Richard the Lionheart, the Knights Templar, Lusignans, and the Venetians, had all tried their best to Latinise Cyprus and rid the island of its Byzantine influence. There was no Orthodox archbishop when the Ottomans took the island, and any remaining Orthodox bishops and priests were living in stark poverty in rural villages. Many Orthodox churches and monasteries from Byzantine Greek rule had been confiscated, and some had been fully converted to Catholic churches.

---

[1] (Oberling, 1982, p. 4)

The Turks rivals at the time however, were the Venetians, so it was now the Latin church which suffered oppression and higher taxes under Ottoman rule and the Greek Orthodox church which flourished.

The millet system meant that the Greek Orthodox people were given their own autonomy and their own laws and court systems. This led to the reinstatement of the Archbishop of Cyprus, who under Ottoman rule became not just a religious leader but the ethnic leader of the Greek Cypriots. The Ottoman Turks promoted this, looking for someone to take responsibility for the loyalty of the Greek Orthodox population. This power, given to the Archbishop by the Turkish rulers, would go on to become very relevant in the 20th century.

The relationship between the Orthodox and Ottoman elites was good throughout this time. The Orthodox Church even pushed in 1670 for the island to come under direct control of the head of the Ottoman Navy, as they thought it would help the island regain some importance after the Ottoman conquest of Crete. The Ottoman empire indeed did change the administrative status of the island in response.

The Orthodox (later Greek Cypriot) population and Muslim (later Turkish Cypriot) population also got on well. They lived in the same villages and interacted in

21

daily life. The communities even cooperated in uprisings together, mainly in protest against tax burdens and against both the Greek Orthodox clergy and the Turkish Ottoman rulers.

Historians such as Jan-Erik Smilden question whether the Greek Orthodox church would have survived at all had the Ottoman Turks not come to the island in 1571, and saved the Greek population from Venetian serfdom and oppression.[1]

Cyprus as a British protectorate

During the 19th Century, having to fight against both the Greek uprisings of the 1820s and damaging wars with the increasingly powerful Russians, the Ottoman empire started to lose power and influence. The under-pressure Ottomans, in their desperation, had offered to lend Cyprus to the British three times during this period - in 1833, 1841, and 1845.[2] The Brits turned them down on all three occasions, having very little interest in the island until 1869. In 1869, the Suez Canal opened, providing better trade links from the British isles to, amongst other places, India - the jewel in the crown of the British empire. Cyprus's newly

---

[1] (Smilden, 2007)
[2] (Kadioğlu, 2010)

convenient location, near the opening of the new canal, became of great interest to the Brits.

In 1877 the Russians defeated the Ottomans in war and roughly drafted the terms for the Treaty of San Stefano. The idea was to finalise the treaty in a meeting of the world powers at the Congress of Berlin in 1878. On 4th June 1878 though, shortly before the Congress opened on the 13th June, it was announced that the British and the Ottomans had come to a secret agreement in the meantime - the Cyprus Convention. The Turks ceded administration of the island to the British, and in exchange, the British promised to use the island as a base to protect the Turks against aggression from Russia. This deal gave the defeated Ottomans protection from the Russians, and allowed the Brits to protect their interests in India and the Suez Canal. It also aided Britain in their attempts to quell the ever growing power of the Russian Empire. The agreement also allowed for the Turks to claim that the situation was temporary in order to save face.[1]

---

[1] (American University, 1964, p. 38)

Life on the British-leased island

The Cypriot population, both Turkish Sunni Muslims and Greek Orthodox Christians, didn't take to the island's new occupiers. The biggest symbol of British oppression on the island was the 'Cyprus Tribute'. British-administered Cyprus had to pay the Ottoman empire tribute in exchange for administering an island that still technically fell under Ottoman sovereignty. This annual fixed payment from the British to the Turks was negotiated to be approximately 92,800 pounds sterling. As well as Cyprus having to pay this, they also had to pay for the expenditure of the British administration, which was much more lavish than the previous Ottoman expenditure.[1] These outgoings were a steady drain on Cyprus's already struggling economy, and left nothing for internal improvements to the island or the lives of the population.

In 1889 a group headed by the Greek Orthodox Archbishop, a position considered to be the ethnic leader of the Greek Cypriots since Ottoman times, visited the Queen to talk about the fiscal burden on the island. It was obvious the Queen would do nothing to

---

[1] (American University, 1964, p. 37)

alleviate this burden, but Archbishop Sophronios did have his purpose diverted by instead being awarded an honorary Doctor of Divinity degree by the University of Oxford.[1]

What annoyed both the Ottoman Turks and the Cypriots even more was that the tribute wasn't even paid to the Ottoman empire, but instead deposited straight in the Bank of England to pay off an old Ottoman loan from 1855.

In 1907 even Winston Churchill, the Undersecretary of State for the Colonies at the time, visited Cyprus and wrote in his subsequent report:

"We have no right whatever, except by force majeure, to take a penny of the Cyprus tribute to relieve us from our own just obligations, however unfortunately contracted. There is scarcely any spectacle more detestable than the oppression of a small community by a great Power for the purpose of pecuniary profit; and that is, in fact, the spectacle which our own financial treatment of Cyprus at this moment indisputably presents."[2]

---

[1] (American University, 1964, p. 38)

[2] (Hill, 2010)

The tribute caused huge agitation and resentment towards the British and was continually used as a symbol of British oppression on the island.

RISING GREEK NATIONALISM

In 1914, when the First World War started, the Ottoman Empire joined the Central Powers – the opponents of the British and the allied forces. In response, on 5th November 1918, the Brits annexed Cyprus in to the British Empire.

Cyprus was not the main focus of the British, and the Brits tried to offer Cyprus to Greece a number of times. In 1912 and in 1913, in exchange for a naval base in the Ionian Sea, and several more times in 1915, to try to persuade the Greeks to join the First World War. Greece turned them down on all occasions.

Despite this, agitated by the Cyprus Tribute and the lack of British investment, Greek nationalism amongst the Greek Orthodox population on the island had started to rise under British rule.

An international rise in nationalism

The interwar years were set against an international background of Greco-Turkish tensions, Greek nationalism and the rising idea of enosis (union with Greece) internationally, and were particularly

27

troublesome. The Greek premier had promised his people a "Greece of two continents and five seas"[1] with a view to invading and 'taking back' ex-Byzantine land. In contrast, Atatürk was very anti-expansionist in the way he founded and ran the Republic of Turkey, coining and ruling by the phrase "peace at home and peace abroad"[2].

In 1923, at the end of a tough war between Greece and Turkey, the Greek prime minister requested an enforced population exchange with Turkey, which Turkey accepted. Cyprus had already been ceded to the British and so was not a part of this exchange. The agreement asserted that "Greek subjects, who belonged to the Muslim faith" would be exchanged with "Turkish subjects of the Greek Orthodox faith"[3]. This population switch was notable in that it meant that both Greeks and Turks had officially recognised their religion as one of the most important parts of their nationality. Religion, and whether you were Sunni Muslim or Orthodox Christian, would later go on to become an extremely important factor in deciding the community you were part of in Cyprus.

---

[1] (Oberling, 1982, p. 23)
[2] (Oberling, 1982, p. 51)
[3] (Cagaptay, 2005, p. 83)

Internationally, the concept of enosis and the Megali Idea was rising in islands with a high proportion of Greek Orthodox ex-Byzantine subjects. The Megali Idea was the idea that the Eastern Roman Byzantine empire should be revived and the land taken back by the Greek Orthodox people. In time it lead to Greek uprisings across Europe, eventually even leading to the formation of the state of Greece.

The Greek Uprising of 1821 happened across the continent in places like Crete and Macedonia. Greek-speaking people in these islands rose up and slaughtered Turkish neighbours in their villages[1] in the name of the Megali Idea. Some of the violence also made its way to Cyprus, where it was dealt with effectively and swiftly by the Ottomans. While the uprising did somewhat sour good relations between the Greeks and Turks in Cyprus (the sultan in Istanbul had initially outright refused to allow any executions of Greek rebels, before eventually giving permission to execute 486 people) good relations were restored quickly between Cypriots of all languages and religions.[2] During the Ottoman reform period, the Tanzimat in the late 1830s, the power of the Orthodox

---

[1] (Oberling, 1982, p. 44)
[2] (Smilden, 2007)

Church was even strengthened by the Turks, and given more power than it had had even before the uprising. The outcome in other islands though, was tragically different.

Cypriot similarities to Crete

The Greek uprising in Crete was not as well handled as in Cyprus, and ended in the Muslim minority on the island being almost entirely wiped out.

Crete has a very similar historical background to Cyprus. It was Byzantine, Arab-Byzantine, Venetian, Ottoman and then taken under the control of Western powers and the UK in the 19th Century, closely mirroring the history of Cyprus. Crete also, when Western powers took over, had a Byzantine-descended Greek-speaking Orthodox Christian majority and a significant Turkish-speaking Sunni Muslim minority population and so, in the 18th century, a very similar cultural makeup to Cyprus. The major difference between the two islands is that in Cyprus any talk of reunification in 1821 was squashed quickly and relations between the Turks and the Greeks on the island continued positively, whilst Crete was to be taken by Greece, with any Muslims wiped out.

In 1897 Greek troops distributed guns to Christian villagers and instructed them to exterminate their Muslim neighbours.[1] The result was brutal. Around 1000 Cretan Turks[2] were massacred, and around 4000 were displaced as refugees, losing homes and properties. The massacres were covered up by the Cretan authorities at the time. Investigations were ordered, but the British Vice-Consul in Candia – Lysimachos Kalokairinos – helped to ensure that no Muslims were included in the investigation party[3] and the investigation subsequently reported that there was no trace of any massacre at all. The 4000 Cretan Turk refugees, after losing their homes, businesses, and seeing their friends and family murdered were told outright that their allegations were false.

It was only a short time later that Sir Alfred Biliotti, the Britsh consul, confirmed the massacre, finding evidence of the massacres of not just adults, but of at least 201 male and 173 female children.[4]

Arthur Evans - a renowned British archeologist, who had been in Crete for many years - wrote in the Manchester Guardian in 1898:

---

[1] (Barchard, 2006, p. 27)
[2] (Barchard, 2006, p. 28)
[3] (Barchard, 2006, p. 29)
[4] (Barchard, 2006, p. 30)

"The most deliberate act of extermination was that perpetrated at Eteà. In this small village, too, the Moslem inhabitants, including the women and children, had taken refuge in the mosque, which the men defended for a while. The building itself is a solid structure, but the door of the small walled enclosure... was finally blown in, and the defenders laid down their arms, understanding, it would appear, that their lives were to be spared. Men, women and children, they were all led forth to the church of St. Sophia, which lies on a hill about half an hour above the village, and then and there dispatched—the men cut to pieces, the women and children shot. A young girl who had fainted, and was left for dead, alone lived to tell the tale."[1]

An eye witness, a woman from the village of Roukaka, gave the following deposition to French officials:

"Christians threw Halime, the pregnant wife of Huseyin Mehmedakis, on the ground and slit open her belly, taking the foetus out. They also knifed Fatime, daughter of Mustafa Omer Efendakis, cutting her open from her breasts to the middle of her back. They pushed the men into the mosque and, as they killed them, hurled them from the minaret, which they then set ablaze with gasoline. Dogs were running all over the village carrying half-burnt hands

---

[1] (Gere, 2010, pp. 71-72)

and feet. The children were stabbed to death, and a few were crushed beneath the minaret when it collapsed."[1]

In the years following, remaining Muslims fled the island of Crete, and in 1908 the island was unified with Greece.

The rise of enosis in Cyprus

Back in Cyprus, Greek nationalism had also been gradually rising from the start of the century, with British rule being far less amenable to the Cypriots than Turkish rule had been.[2]

Greek diplomats in British Cyprus would try their best to evoke nationalist feelings amongst Orthodox Cypriots. Orthodox schools were turned in to indoctrination centres for Greek nationalism, with the Ministry of Education in Greece sending fervently nationalist school teachers to teach on the island.[3] The British inspector of schools reported of worrying anti-Turkish sentiments in Cypriot schools at the time, citing the pupils being taught war songs against the Turks.[4] National youth clubs were also set up by the

---

[1] (Oberling, 1982, p. 45)
[2] (Newsinger, 2015, p. 89)
[3] (Oberling, 1982, p. 15)
[4] (Oberling, 1982, p. 20)

Greeks to help harness a nationalist feeling in the young.[1]

The greatest failure of the British though, was that they allowed the standard of living in Cyprus to decline so sharply for the local population under their rule, leaving people desperately poor and looking for alternatives. The Turkish Cypriots were getting poorer too, causing thousands to emigrate to Turkey for work and education.[2]

In 1931, one Greek Orthodox bishop issued a manifesto demanding unification with Greece[3] - causing a week of riots and the burning down of Government House by Greek agitators. The British had sent reinforcements and suppressed the outbreak - killing 11 people and expelling many more from the island. The British responded by making any calls for enosis (the idea that Cyprus should be unified with the country of Greece) illegal, banning the flying of the Greek flag, imposing large fines, and even for a while prohibiting the ringing of the Orthodox church bells.

During the 1940s, most resistance to British rule came from the Greek Cypriot communist party - the

---

[1] (Oberling, 1982, p. 34)
[2] (Oberling, 1982, p. 53)
[3] (Newsinger, 2015, p. 90)

Progressive Party of the Working Class (AKEL) - who at the time were the most powerful political force on the island. They had not been campaigning for enosis, but for self governance. AKEL organised a number of protests, and in response, in 1945 the Brits arrested and jailed a number of trade unionists and communists.[1]

Later in the decade, the tide begun to turn against AKEL. The nationalist right wing established a new party (the Cyprus National Party) as well as the Cyprus Farmers' Union (PEK) and gained the support of the Greek Orthodox church. The church came out openly in favour of these nationalist right wing parties, in favour of enosis, and firmly against communism and the trade unions. The church even provided scab labour[2] to break miners strikes in 1948 to undermine the left wing parties.

With the tide turning against them, AKEL quickly changed its position on the national question, abandoning its stance that Cyprus should be an independent self-governing country, and instead also coming out in favour of enosis. They approached the church in 1950, hoping to present a united front with

---

[1] (Newsinger, 2015, p. 90)
[2] (Newsinger, 2015, p. 90)

them, and suggesting an unofficial plebiscite on the idea of enosis. The church refused to work with the party, but instead organised their own enosis plebiscite independently in Greek Orthodox churches across the island, claiming that an overwhelming majority of people were in favour.

The Brits, of course, ignored this plebiscite. The Foreign Secretary (and future Prime Minister) Sir Anthony Eden, even went so far as to angrily rebuff the Greek Prime Minister when asked about it, remarking that New York also had a large Greek population and so asking why Greece were not also claiming that.[1] Makarios III - who would very soon after become the church's vehemently pro-enosis archbishop and go on to become absolutely pivotal to the resistance movements against the British - was the man behind this plebiscite.

---

[1] (Newsinger, 2015, p. 92)

When the charismatic and popular Makarios III, aged 37, was elected archbishop in 1950, he immediately set about consolidating[1] the position of the nationalist right wing. He also set about strengthening the office of archbishop as the religious and political leader of the Greek Cypriot population - as it had once been during Ottoman times.

Archbishop Makarios in 1962

World Telegram & Sun photo by O. Fernandez

In stark contrast, Turkish Cypriots were and are some of the most secular Muslims in the world. They have been found to be hardly "influenced by organized religion, rarely attend mosques, and adhere to a very strict form of secularism"[2] and had no clear religious leader to rally behind.

---

[1] (Newsinger, 2015, p. 91)
[2] (Yeşilada, 2009)

THE RISE OF EOKA

In 1945, for the first time in Britain's history, the elections were won by the left-wing Labour Party – a party whose ideology was incompatible with colonialism. Between 1945 and 1951, the Labour government – most notable for creating the British National Health Service - granted independence to India, Burma and Sri Lanka, before declaring that the gradual liberation of all British colonies was just a matter of time. Two of the Labour Party's leaders – Ernest Bevin and Herbert Morrison – continuously stressed that the existence of colonies was an 'embarrassment' for a left-wing party in government.

Makarios did not want the independence for Cyprus that the Brits were offering though – he wanted enosis with Greece. So in July 1952, during a visit to Greece, Makarios set up a secret 'committee of liberation' to plan and prepare for the clandestine subversive struggle for enosis.

Archbishop Makarios believed, at this time, that enosis would be achieved mainly through diplomatic efforts and international pressure on the British. Nevertheless, he involved the infamous Georgios

38

Grivas when forming his committee, a tough and violent retired Greek Army officer with very extreme right wing nationalist politics.[1]

Georgios Grivas was of Cypriot origins, but had moved to Greece in 1916, took Greek citizenship, and joined the Greek army - fighting in both world wars. In 1952, after a reconnaissance of Cyprus under instruction from the committee, Grivas formed the belief that enosis would be achieved through a protracted, bloody and violent guerrilla war that would take years before victory was achieved. This was in contrast to Makarios' original plans, which favoured minimising any needless loss of life, and consisted of a short campaign of sabotage and public disorder to pressure the Brits.

Grivas was in no position to challenge the more diplomatic and less violent strategy of the archbishop, and so initially accepted his outlook, but in 1954 went about setting up the National Organisation of Cypriot Fighters (EOKA) to carry out his own strategy in the event that a less violent approach wouldn't work.

Grivas assumed the nom de guerre Digenis, in reference to the Byzantine legends of Digenis Akritas,

---

[1] (Newsinger, 2015, p. 92)

and recruited his second in command - Grigoris Afxentiou. Afxentiou, like Grivas, was born in Cyprus but had left for Greece. He was unsuccessful in his attempts to join the Greek military academy in Athens, but joined instead as a volunteer, before being discharged and returning to Cyprus in 1952 to help his father with his business, working in the fields and as a taxi driver.[1] Grivas appreciated his background in the Greek military and bold nationalist views, and recruited him as his right hand man.

Grivas also recruited militant fighters from the right-wing Cyprus Farmers' Union (PEK) and the two main youth movements – the Church-controlled Christian Youth Movement (OHEN) and the nationalist Pancyprian Youth Movement (PEON). Grivas intended to turn the youth of Cyprus "into the seedbed of EOKA"[2] and would go on to use mostly youth members of the organisation in planned terrorist attacks in towns and cities across Cyprus. Grivas' recruitment of schoolchildren for his cause was seen as an easy way of tying down the police and exposing the British establishment to criticism for any actions they might take against "mere schoolchildren"[3]. The United States

---

[1] (Chrysopoulos, 2018)
[2] (British Counterinsurgency, 2015, p. 94)
[3] (Holland R. F., 1994, p. 186)

Congress noted in 1974 that children had played an "extraordinarily militant"[1] role in EOKA. Grivas used these children astutely, putting them in harms way when it was politically or militarily expedient to do so.

Children were involved in riots and stone-throwing against police, but also threw bombs and carried out assassinations for Grivas. Bombs were thrown by youngsters at British personnel houses, police stations and army camps.[2]

Georgios Grivas in 1967

Dutch National Archives
2.24.01.04/9 20-8717

EOKA attacks begin

By the end of March, EOKA had started a full campaign of bombings, mostly in the major cities. On 1st April 1955, Grivas, keeping his involvement secret, claimed responsibility for these terrorist attacks in a declaration signed with the name Digenis.

With Grivas as the military leader, and Makarios as political and religious leader, these attacks marked the start of the armed struggle for enosis by the EOKA organisation.

---

[1] (United States. Congress. Senate. Committee on the Judiciary. Subcommittee to Investigate Problems Connected with Refugees and Escapees, 1974)
[2] (French, 2015, pp. 86-88)

The British had been surprised by these attacks and quickly responded by strengthening their military bases on the island with troops from Egypt.

By the end of April, EOKA attacks were briefly suspended, allowing them time to recruit and organise more potential child soldiers. ANE (Valiant Youth of EOKA) was set up - a pupil's group with a branch in every school in Cyprus - to these ends.[1]

Further attacks were carried out by EOKA on June 19th, including grenade and bomb attacks on military installations, homes of senior officials and police stations. In one bombing, EOKA managed to demolish Famagusta police headquarters.

These assassinations of the police are notable as they followed the tactical playbook of other terrorist groups at the time. David C Rapoport, "one of the founding figures of terrorism studies"[2], has compared EOKA's tactical systematic assassinations of the police to the tactics used by the similarly anti-colonial anti-British IRA in Ireland. He theorizes that these tactics are fairly common in what he calls the "second wave" of terrorism, and also notes similarities in the way that

---

[1] (Richter, Geschichte der Insel Zypern, 2006, p. 254)
[2] (Horgan & Braddock, 2012, p. 1)

both groups took money, weapons and volunteers from foreign sympathisers for their causes against the British (the IRA from Irish Americans, and the "Greek" Cypriots from Greece). Rapoport notes that, after attacks on the local police force, "military units would replace them and would prove too clumsy to cope without producing counter-atrocities, increasing social support for the terrorists"[1], which was especially effective considering that Grivas recruited mostly children, especially in urban areas.

The British realised they were losing their handle on the situation in Cyprus, and as well as the extra troops they'd stationed on the island, responded with diplomatic manoeuvring. This largely involved trying to play the Greek and Turkish governments off against each other, using the Turkish Cypriot minority and Turkish government as the means to prevent enosis.[2] The British Foreign Secretary, Anthony Eden, saw Turkey as "the key to protecting British interests"[3] in Cyprus. Tensions between the two communities were stoked by the British administrations recruitment of mostly Turkish Cypriot policemen to fight EOKA. By the start of 1956, the Cypriot police force was

---

[1] (Rapoport, 2013, pp. 282-310)
[2] (Newsinger, 2015, p. 111)
[3] (Newsinger, 2015, p. 97)

dominated by over 4000 Turkish Cypriots, compared to under 1000 Greek Cypriots, all very much on the front line fighting EOKA terrorists.

The British also exerted influence on the Turkish prime minster Adnan Menderes, successfully turning the Cyprus issue from a British colonial issue to a Turkish-Greek one. When Turkish Cypriots visited the British minister of foreign affairs and requested that Cyprus remain a colony instead of giving in to the calls for enosis (Cypriot muslims were afraid that they would be massacred by Greek nationalists, as they were in Crete), the British minister allegedly replied: "You should not be asking for colonialism at this day and age, you should be asking for Cyprus be returned to Turkey, its former owner"[1]. Turkey hadn't wanted to get involved in the Cyprus problem at first, but the Greek and British diplomatic manoeuvring and increasing Greek military involvement in an island just off the south coast of Turkish land eventually forced their hand.[2]

---

[1] (Tahsin, 2001, p. 38)
[2] (Oberling, 1982, p. 60)

By the end of September 1955, with EOKA attacks against the British worsening, the British administration decided to replace the British Governor of Cyprus, Sir Robert Perceval Armitage, and instead appointed Sir John Alan Francis Harding – a battle-hardened British military man.

Sir John Harding

Harding-Makarios negotiations

When Harding arrived in Cyprus on October 3rd, his priorities were both to increase security, and come to a diplomatic solution. On November 26th, after 41 bombs exploded on the 19th and two British soldiers were killed on the 24th[1], he declared a state of emergency and proceeded with British large scale search operations, which did sometimes find arms caches or result in arrests, but also served to alienate Greek Cypriots whose homes had been searched. With the cold war and the global fight against communism ongoing, the governor also saw fit to ban the communist party AKEL and detain 128 of its leading members, crippling the only political party in Cyprus

---

[1] (Novo, 2015, p. 91)

that opposed EOKA.[1] The unintended result of all of this was that sympathy for EOKA was increased amongst the Greek Cypriot community, assisting them in their recruitment efforts. Priests and teachers, under strict secrecy, were scouting for young men aged 14-24, and were mostly successful.[2]

Alongside of all this, Harding had started diplomatic negotiations with the Greek Cypriot archbishop Makarios, commencing what became known as the Harding-Makarios negotiations, to discuss the situation on the island.

Archbishop Makarios was difficult throughout the talks, and with EOKA terrorist attacks and violence continuing even while Harding and Makarios actively negotiated, Harding developed a "personal distaste" for Makarios. Makarios was also pedantic and difficult in negotiations, annoying the more direct Harding. [3]

The British were annoyed throughout these talks at Makarios' maximalist approach to negotiations, and what they saw as his stubborn refusal to compromise. The Brits were in fact quite limited in what they could offer the Greek Cypriots, as they couldn't be seen

---

[1] (Newsinger, 2015, p. 99)
[2] (Richter, History of Cyprus: Volume 2, 2011, pp. 706-707)
[3] (Novo, 2015, pp. 92-93)

46

internationally to be giving in to terrorists, especially considering that the British didn't want to sour their relationship with Turkey.[1]

The most contentious point of negotiation from the beginning was the rights of the Turkish Cypriots. Makarios categorically refused to accept the reality that enosis would be unacceptable to the Turkish Cypriots and Turkey. The British Foreign Office became irritated with the Greek nationalist's refusal to accept a fundamental factor (Turkey) in the negotiations, and frustrated that Makarios could not come to terms with Turkey's "genuine and strong" interest in the island and his inability to "acknowledge the existence of a distinct Turkish Cypriot community who remained directly opposed to enosis"[2]. Makarios would repeatedly ask to exclude Turkey from any negotiations, and even asked for concessions that would exclude from the cabinet of any future government of Cyprus any Cypriot national who considered themselves 'Turkish Cypriot'.

These problems around Makarios's dislike for Turks and Turkish Cypriots all became more pronounced in January 1956. On Grivas's explicit orders, EOKA had

---

[1] (Novo, 2015, p. 90)
[2] (Novo, 2015, p. 96)

avoided conducting operations on Turkish Cypriot victims. In January, Grivas changed his mind, ordering the assassination of a Turkish Cypriot police sergeant[1], having him shot in the chest as he was driving back to his home in Paphos. This only served to reinforce the fears of Turkish Cypriot people regarding their insecurity on the island, putting Britain in no mood for concessions that would upset Turkey further.

While Makarios and Harding tried to agree on a constitution for a self-determining Cypriot state, Harding even wrote to Makarios, on the 14th February 1956: "It must be recognised that persistent violence and disorder have increased the difficulties of introducing constitutional government. Fear of intimidation has stifled free expression of opinion. The minorities are more concerned than before about the possible consequences for them of the advent of self-government"

In the end though, the final straw for the British was not discrimination against the Turks, but EOKA itself. With Makarios and Harding on the brink of an agreement; Makarios, as a result of a consultation with Grivas on 28th January 1956, demanded new

---

[1] (Novo, 2015, p. 94)

concessions, one of which was to grant amnesty to all political offenders in Cyprus. London felt that Makarios was, at such a late stage, moving the goalposts, concluding in Cabinet that: "[a]t this final stage, however, the Archbishop had put the agreement in jeopardy by asking for an amnesty for all political offenders in Cyprus."[1]

The British Secretary of State for the Colonies, Lennox-Boyd (who believed strongly in decolonisation and was responsible for granting independence to Ghana, Iraq, Malaya and Sudan) informed Makarios that he would agree to some of the new concessions in exchange for Makarios's condemnation of violence and his aid in restoring peace in Cyprus. He even agreed to pardon EOKA criminals "except those involving violence against the person or the illegal possession of arms, ammunition or explosives". His statement demonstrated the British government's willingness to compromise and reach an agreement with the Greek-Cypriots. Makarios refused, and in his statement replied that he could not accept that EOKA members arrested for possession of arms and explosives would not be granted amnesty. The British, frustrated with Makarios's lack of cooperation and his

---

[1] (Novo, 2015, p. 100)

refusal to denounce terrorism, took the latest rejection as a sign that a deal would never be agreed and pulled out of negotiations. Harding confronted Makarios, telling him that if he would not compromise at all then violence in Cyprus would continue. Harding is said to have found the Archbishop's response "illuminating". Harding wrote to his son on the 4th March: "By his persistent refusal to denounce violence the Archbishop forces us to the conclusion that he believes in violence as a political weapon and would not hesitate to use it again—a curious attitude for a so-called Christian leader."

On 9th March, Harding secured approval from the British government to have Makarios deported for his links to, and refusal to denounce, EOKA terrorism. Makarios was taken in to custody while attempting to board a flight fleeing to Athens. Three other men were also arrested, including a leading recruiter for EOKA youth groups, and the four men were sent to exile in the Seychelles.

The violence continues

After Makarios's exile, and with Grivas now essentially in charge, violence on the island became worse. EOKA started a campaign of house bombings, strikes, riots, ambushes and raids on police stations. In April and May they were killing an average of 2 people a week.

In January 1957 Grivas decided to begin systematically attacking the Turkish Cypriot population, intentionally sparking intercommunal tensions and rioting, and therefore making life more difficult for British troops.[1]

Many Turkish Cypriot citizens in mixed villages were chased out of their home by their Greek Cypriot neighbours around this time, ultimately leading to the first instances of physical separation between the two communities.[2]

The Greek Cypriot municipal councils were also helping to Hellenise the island, changing street names to Greek alternatives and ridding the island of any Muslim history. They removed tombs of notable Muslims in 'street widening' projects and allowed only the Greek national flag to fly at the town halls in Cyprus.[3]

---

[1] (French, 2015, p. 258)
[2] (Oberling, 1982, p. 61)
[3] (Oberling, 1982, p. 56)

Grivas also killed many Greek Cypriot civilians, mainly for his belief that they had spoken to the police (even if they had only spoken under interrogation), or for their politics. Members of the AKEL party were targeted[1] as were any left wing civilians who dared question the idea that Makarios was the sole leader of the Greek-Cypriot community. These killings for what Grivas considered to be treason usually took place in public.[2]

In March 1957, Harding agreed a truce with Grivas, which lasted nearly a year.

In December of 1957, Sir Hugh Foot was assigned the British Governor of Cyprus. It was thought that his more liberal background might work better than Harding's military background in winning popular support with the locals.

---

[1] (Holland R. , 1998, p. 203)
[2] (Holland R. , 1998, p. 148)

THE FORMATION OF THE REPUBLIC OF CYPRUS

In the meantime Harold Macmillan had taken over as Prime Minister of Great Britain, and immediately looked to withdraw Britain from the situation he had referred to in his memoirs as the "Cyprus tangle"[1]. A general election was due in 1959 and the Conservative government wanted a plan in place before then so that the issue wasn't exploited during election campaigning by the opposing Labour Party. He drew up the Macmillan Plan, whereby Cyprus would be jointly administered by Turkey, Greece and the UK, in what he saw as a good compromise for both the Turkish and Greek Cypriot communities. When the plan was debated in the House of Commons on 26th June 1958, it garnered healthy cross-party support across both the governing party and the opposition, and was seen internationally as a positive move by the British.[2]

Makarios, now exiled in Greece, refused the plan at first, still pushing for full enosis. But on 7th September

---

[1] (Varnava, 2010, p. 2)
[2] (French, 2015, p. 270 and 282)

he privately told the Greek government he might accept Macmillan's offer of independence, given the British determination to go ahead with their plan regardless. He still wasn't happy with the proposed involvement of the Turks, even trying to stop Turkish representatives from being involved in talks. In letters, Makarios had explained that he was willing to accept independence rather than enosis because he "had to face up to the situation realistically", also mentioning his fears that not accepting independence from the British quickly would "inevitably lead to partition, or would give the Turks rights which it would impossible (even under different conditions) to remove later"[1].

There were signs that there were even some EOKA leaders who welcomed Makarios' declaration that he would accept the plan. Documents ceased by the British showed senior member Kyriakos Matsis insisting to group leaders that "all should follow the Archbishop's new line". Security forces ceased similar letters written by EOKA district leaders in the Troodos mountains.[2]

Grivas however, was furious with the plan and saw independence as an unacceptable compromise,

---

[1] (French, 2015, p. 272)
[2] (French, 2015, p. 283)

believing it opened the door to taksim (a partitioned Cyprus) and reduced the chances of ever being able to hand the whole island to Greece. In response, he stepped up violence on the island, ordering his guerillas to "strike indiscriminately at every English person wherever they can be found"[1]. His militia started to attack and murder not just policemen and soldiers but British civilians and expats of any age or gender. Sir Hugh Foot had to flood the main towns with military patrols and supply pistols to any British civilians who wanted them. Grivas also sent leaflets threatening violence to anyone, Greek or otherwise, that spoke out against EOKA, and intensified attacks on Greek Cypriot 'traitors' in the summer of 1958.

Cypriots were divided by Grivas' determination to fight on, and welcomed his partial truce in August, although they would have liked it to extend to members of their own community. When Grivas enforced a boycott of British goods on the island, and with the Archbishop and ethnarch Makarios starting to take a softer and less violent position than the EOKA leader, EOKA started to lose the broad support of the Greek Cypriot community.[2]

---

[1] (French, 2015, p. 274)
[2] (French, 2015, p. 284)

Special branch reported at the time that "the Greek Cypriot population are heartily sick of EOKA whose activities result in curfews and financial hardship" and noted that "merchants have been openly cursing EOKA for its lack of consideration for the welfare of the people"[1].

In 1959 the London-Zurich agreements were drawn up and agreed by the Turkish, Greek and British government. Makarios brought an advisory body to London with him to approve the agreements. The group consisted of a number of personalities drawn wide from Greek Cypriot political parties, even including politicians from the left. With EOKA support waning, he notably didn't include any representatives of EOKA, annoying Grivas.[2]

Turkish Cypriot leader
Dr. Fazıl Küçük

In February 1959, Makarios signed the London-Zurich agreements on behalf of the Greek Cypriot community, and Dr. Fazıl Küçük signed them on behalf of the Turkish Cypriot community. Dr Küçük – a medical doctor who had studied in Paris, Switzerland

---

[1] (French, 2015, p. 285)
[2] (Karyos, 2009, p. 15)

and Turkey and had become the de-facto leader of the Turkish Cypriot community – went on to become the first Turkish Cypriot vice president of the bi-communal Republic of Cyprus.

The Republic of Cyprus was formed in 1960, with rights of self-determination for both the Turkish Cypriot and Greek Cypriot communities on the island. The agreements provided guarantor powers for the nations of Britain, Greece and Turkey in the case that they would need to need to take action (military or otherwise) to maintain the "aim of re-establishing the state of affairs [i.e. bi-communal consociational state] created by the present Treaty"[1]. Each guarantor power was also allowed a set number of military troops based on the island as part of the signed treaties.

---

[1] (Ministry of Foreign Affairs, Republic of Cyprus, 1960)

THE ISLAND SPLITS INTO TWO

Peace in the new bi-communal republic of Cyprus didn't last long. Greek nationalism and the desire for enosis had gained momentum now amongst the Greek Cypriot community, and was difficult to stop even after the island gained its independence. Makarios and the Greek Cypriot leadership soon begun looking for ways to decrease the constitutional powers and protections afforded to the Turkish Cypriot minority.

Makarios employed ex-EOKA terrorists as government ministers, and gave inflammatory speeches to the Greek Cypriot community, telling his Greek Orthodox followers that "the realization of our hopes and realizations is not complete under the London and Zurich agreements" and stating that "Greek Cypriots must continue to march forward to complete the work begun by EOKA heroes". On September 1962, he said in a speech:

"Unless this small Turkish community forming a part of the Turkish race which has been the terrible enemy of

Hellenism is expelled, the duty of the heroes of EOKA can never be considered as terminated."[1]

Even Cypriot schools and government television channels pushed an anti-Turkish pro-Greek agenda. British journalist Michael Wall reported that Cypriot children were being taught that "Cyprus is Greek – and that the Turks are intruders"[2].

The Akritas Plan

In 1963 the Akritas Plan was drawn up in secret by the Greek Cypriot minister of the interior Yorgadjis, a close associate of Makarios[3] who had been a fanatical EOKA terrorist before 1960, and who had publicly declared in 1962 as a member of the government that "There is no place in Cyprus for anyone who is not Greek"[4]. The main points of his plan were to 1) remove the protective concessions given to the Turkish Cypriot community in the constitution, and 2) remove the Treaty of Guarantee and Treaty of Alliance, allowing the Greek Cypriot leadership to do as they pleased without interference from Turkey or Britain.

---

[1] (Oberling, 1982, p. 68)
[2] (Oberling, 1982, p. 69)
[3] (Solsten, 1991, p. 34)
[4] (Oberling, 1982, p. 68)

The ultimate aim of the plan was that enosis would become possible again, as would the defeat and extermination of the Turkish Cypriots. This would be the beginning of the Greek 'final solution' for the Turks, has been described as a "blueprint for genocide"[1] and was widely perceived as a plan for the ethnic cleansing of the Turkish-speaking Muslim community on the island.

The extent to which Makarios was fully committed to the secretive Akritas Plan (which was leaked in 1966 by a pro-Grivas Greek Cypriot newspaper) is unclear, but in November 1963 Makarios put forward a list of 13 changes to the constitution, very much in line with the first stages of the plan. Frank Hoffmeister (former UN Special Advisor on Cyprus) notes that, in general, "the resemblance of political and military steps in the plan and in reality is striking"[2].

Violence begins again

Greek police would stop and search Turkish Cypriots frequently around the Turkish quarters during this time by armed Greek Cypriot civilians hired as 'special constables', on orders from Interior Minister

---

[1] (Bryant & Papadakis, 2012, p. 249)
[2] (Hoffmeister, 2006)

Yorgacis. Turkish nationalism had grown in response to Greek nationalism, and the TMT (the 'Turkish Resistance Organisation') had been formed as a way to protect the Turks against ongoing Greek oppression.

In the early hours of the 21st December 1963 a Greek Cypriot policeman stopped a taxi in Nicosia, demanding to see the identification papers of Turkish Cypriot passengers making their way home to the Turkish quarter. When the Greek policeman demanded to perform body searches on the female passengers, the Turkish Cypriot driver Zeki Halil stepped in on their behalf and reminded the policeman of their constitutional rights. TMT had instructed Turkish Cypriot civilians to raise their voices and discuss their issues loudly in situations like this, and so Zeki started to do this in line with that advice. A crowd of locals started to form, and the policeman called for backup. One of the arriving Greek policemen shot the taxi driver dead, along with a Turkish Cypriot women attempting to defend him.[1] Eight other locals were also beaten or wounded.[2]

---

[1] (Cambazis, 2014)
[2] (Ker-Lindsay, 2009, p. 24)

Bloody Christmas

The morning after the shooting, the TMT organised protests of Turkish residents in Northern Nicosia with no incidents. The funeral of the two Turkish Cypriot civilians also took place without incident.

But in the evening hours of the 22nd – the first day of a period that would later become known as 'Bloody Christmas' – shooting broke out. Cars sped through Turkish Cypriot villages firing from the windows, including at Turkish Cypriot schools and cars carrying school children.[1] The Turks fired back from minarets in the mosques of Nicosia's Turkish quarter. As the trouble continued, Makarios and the Turkish Cypriot defence minister (representing the Turkish minority) arranged several ceasefires, none of which were honoured. Nikos Sampson, a former EOKA fighter and a man who hated the Turks, took a group of Greek Cypriots in to the Turkish suburbs and slaughtered Turkish Cypriot civilians indiscriminately, including unarmed men, women and children, before burning down homes. He was lavishly praised by the Greek Cypriot press.[2] When Sir Arthur Clark, the British High Commissioner, flew to Cyprus after taking sick leave in

---

[1] (Oberling, 1982, p. 88)
[2] (Oberling, 1982, p. 97)

England, he found "three dead Turkish peasants propped up against his front gate"[1]. Turkish Cypriots were forced out of their houses with threats, shootings and arson, and had their homes smashed and looted. Turkish mosques and hospitals were desecrated. Hundreds of Turkish Cypriot hostages - mostly women and children - were taken and acts of sadism and cruelty were carried out, unpunished. Children were beaten and killed in front of their parents. The imam of Omorphita and his blind son were murdered in their beds by EOKA-B fighters, their bodies riddled with bullets.[2] Many Turkish Cypriot civilians woke up that morning to heavily armed Greeks in their homes, before being tortured, killed and buried in mass graves.

British journalist H Scott Gibbons, who was reporting in Cyprus at the time, reported the following account from one village:

> "Shots rang out, rifle butts smashed against locked doors, people were dragged into the streets.
>
> A 70-year old Turk was awakened by the sound of his front door splintering. Tottering out of his bedroom, he found several young armed men inside the door.
>
> 'Have you any children,' they asked. Bewildered, he replied, 'Yes.'

---

[1] (Borowiec, 2000, p. 56)
[2] (The Guardian, 1999)

'Send them outside,' he was ordered.

His two sons, 19 and 17 years old, and his granddaughter, aged 10 hastily dressed and followed the gunmen outside.

They were lined up outside the cottage wall. The gunmen machinegunned them to death.

In another house, a 13-year old boy had his hands tied behind his knees and was thrown on the floor. While the house was being ransacked, his captors kicked and abused him. Then a pistol was placed at the back of his head and he was shot."[1]

Mrs. Gülsün Salih also provided the following first-hand account:

"It was a cold evening in January 1964, when there was a knock on the door. Before we could open it, the door was kicked open and about a dozen Greek Cypriots armed with rifles and automatic guns rushed in. They grabbed my husband, Salih Mehmet, aged 60, and took him away, saying that they would be taking him to Nicosia. That was the last I saw of my husband and nothing has been heard of him since then."[2]

On 14th January 1964, a reporter for the Italian daily newspaper 'Il Giorno' wrote:

---

[1] (Gibbons, 1969)
[2] (Oberling, 1982, p. 101)

"Discussions start in London; in Cyprus, the terror continues. Right now we are witnessing the exodus of the Turks from their villages. Thousands of people abandoning homes, lands, herds; Greek terrorism is relentless. This time, the rhetoric of the Hellenes and the busts of Plato do not suffice to cover up barbaric and ferocious behaviours. At four o'clock in the afternoon, curfew is imposed on the Turkish villages. Threats, shootings and attempts of arson start as soon as it becomes dark. After the massacre of Christmas that spared neither women, nor children, it is difficult to put up any resistance. British vehicles are shuttling back and forth between the villages and Turkish Cypriot 'ghettos'." [1]

The aftermath of Bloody Christmas

Rauf Denktaş, a leading figure in the TMT, and later president of the TRNC, believed that the events of Bloody Christmas were a premeditated act by Greece. He wrote that Makarios "unleashed his secretly formed armed forces against the Turkish community" and noted that "Greece was hand in glove with the archbishop in this new conspiracy to destroy the Republic of Cyprus" [2]. A number of international journalists agreed with this interpretation of events.

---

[1] (UK Select Committee on Foreign Affairs, 2004)
[2] (Borowiec, 2000, p. 58)

The Washington Post reported on February 16th 1964 that the Makarios government "deliberately provoked the clashes and is bent upon the extermination of the Turkish population"[1], while the British Daily Express extensively documented attempts of genocide against the Turkish Cypriot population during this time.

On Christmas Eve Sir Arthur Clark joined the talks as Britain, Turkey and Greece - the three guarantor powers - called for a truce. On Christmas morning Turkey sent two air force jets screaming low over Nicosia, in support of the Turkish Cypriots and as a warning for the Greeks, and shortly thereafter Makarios agreed to let the British organise a ceasefire. 2700 soldiers from the British bases on the island were redeployed to the most sensitive areas in an attempt to keep the peace. A British-policed buffer zone was decided, which cut through the heart of Nicosia. A British officer hastily marked the dividing line on a map with green ink, and thus was born the "Green Line" which still remains today[2]. The UN was also drafted in to help, and the UNFICYP (United Nations Peacekeeping Force in Cyprus) was formed. In February 1964, the USA State Department official

---

[1] (Safty, 2011, p. 249)
[2] (Borowiec, 2000, p. 57)

George Ball wrote in a letter to the president "The Greek Cypriots do not want a peace-making force, but they just want to be left alone to kill the Turkish Cypriots"[1].

A 1964 report by the UN Security Council found that 25,000 Turkish Cypriots (around a quarter of them) were displaced by the Greek Cypriots during the violent events of Bloody Christmas. The report also found that "in 109 villages, most of them Turkish Cypriot or mixed villages, 527 houses have been destroyed while 2,000 others have suffered damage from looting"[2]. 364 Turkish Cypriots and 174 Greek Cypriots were killed. The report also uncovered other acts of barbarism towards the Turks – for example, the government had kept telephones, electricity and water supply to certain Turkish villages switched off throughout 1964 purposefully, despite there being no problems with these services and despite agreeing with the UN and Turkish Cypriot leaders numerous times that they would be switched back on.[3] A large proportion of the island's Turkish Cypriot community had had to flee to safety and were living in the Turkish quarter of Nicosia in tents and shacks in seriously

---

[1] (Göktepe, 2005, p. 1)
[2] (UN Security Council, 1964)
[3] (UN Security Council, 1964)

overcrowded slum conditions.[1] They were crammed in to around 3% of the island's territory.

A correspondent of 'U.S. News & World Report' visited one of these Turkish slums and reported:

"My first view of the Turkish quarter was not a pretty sight. Houses were riddled with gaping holes. Whole walls had been blasted off many of them.

There were many dead – some still lying where they had been killed."[2]

The Turkish Cypriots observe Bloody Christmas as an important and sombre day in Cypriot history. The Republic of Cyprus still has no such commemoration. Anthropologist Olga Demetriou has discussed how Greek Cypriot textbooks discuss the events of 1963 as a 'Turkish mutiny', and how the Greek Cypriot state discusses the period as a time of Greek victimization "when, in fact, the vast majority of displaced, killed and wounded were Turkish-Cypriots"[3]. She describes this as paralleling strategies of genocide denial, and notes that Greek history books and the states use of this kind of rhetoric has long been used as a way to legitimise human rights violations and silence further violence and aggression against Turkish Cypriots. In 2004,

---

[1] (Solsten, 1991, p. 36)
[2] (Oberling, 1982, p. 107)
[3] (Demetriou, 2014, p. 180)

Greek Cypriot president at the time Tassos Papadopoulos shamelessly claimed that no Turkish Cypriots at all were killed between 1963 and 1974, which lead to media coverage internationally and even to Greek Cypriot media at the time reporting it as a "blatant lie"[1].

After Bloody Christmas, as huge numbers of Turkish Cypriots were forced to give up their homes and land and retreat in to armed enclaves, the fifteen Turkish Cypriot Government Representatives withdrew from the House of Representatives. All Turkish Cypriots holding public office or working in the civil service also withdrew from their posts. The Republic of Cyprus has since claimed that the Turks withdrew from these positions voluntarily, while the Turkish Cypriots maintain that the Greek Cypriots had forcibly ejected them shortly before fundamentally and unilaterally amending the constitution. It is clear that in at least some areas, Turkish Cypriot government workers and representatives were physically prevented from going to work and from entering government buildings.[2] Despite the removal of the Turkish Cypriots from the government of the Republic of Cyprus, UN

---

[1] (Safty, 2011, p. 248)
[2] (Ker-Lindsay, 2009, p. 36)

Security Council Resolution 186 (the resolution which also formed the peacekeeping force) provided international recognition for the Greek Cypriot administration. The Turks set up their own administration – the General Committee, later the Provisional Cyprus Turkish Administration – and thus the island was divided between the two communities, both physically now, as well as politically.

The formation of the National Guard

In 1964 Makarios invited Grivas back to the island from Greece to take control of the newly formed 'National Guard' – an army of Greek and Greek Cypriot fighters far stronger in numbers than was agreed in the 1960 constitution. The National Guard, heavily supplied with weapons and men from Greece, were formed due to the increasing worry that Turkey might intervene in response to the ongoing treatment of Turkish Cypriots on the island.

Turkish Minister of Foreign Affairs, İhsan Sabri Çağlayangil, said of the National Guard in January 1967:

"As we know, after the 1963 December 'events', the Greek Cypriot Administration oppressed the Turkish community in Cyprus by increasing her military forces

which are much higher than the level foreseen in the Constitution and equipped her army with various guns which were especially imported from Greece. In addition, from July of 1964 a Greek force of ten thousand people had come to the island with full equipment and, in March 1965, the heavy weapons, including tanks, were delivered to the Greek Cypriot Administration."[1]

Grivas, who had of course been instrumental in the EOKA terrorist groups struggle for enosis, immediately stepped up his oppression of the Turkish Cypriots. In between heavily armed attacks on Turkish slums, he begun ordering armed patrols to limit the freedom of movement of people and supplies in and out of Turkish Cypriot strongholds.

Ankara was furious, and ordered Air Force attacks on Greek National Guard positions.[2] Turkey even came close to invading in 1964 in order to permanently restore peace for the Turkish Cypriots, and may have done so if not for a blunt and threatening letter on 5th June 1964 from the US president Lyndon Johnson who, worried about a war between NATO allies Greece and Turkey at the height of the Cold War, warned the Turks off the idea of military intervention.

---

[1] (Coşkun, 2015, p. 22)
[2] (Oberling, 1982, p. 118)

THE GREEK MILITARY JUNTA

On the 21st April 1967, the democratic government of Greece was overthrown by a group of far-right army officers who subsequently ran the country as a right-wing xenophobic dictatorship, in a coup d'etat in which they arrested over 10,000 Greek people. The Junta turned Greece in to a brutal police state where they detained, intimidated and tortured their citizens and political opponents, throwing them in to prison camps without trial.[1] The Council of Europe implored Greece to reinstate both democracy and the Greek constitution immediately after the coup, even before further complaints regarding Greece were brought to the Council of Europe's Human Rights Committee. Norway, Sweden, Denmark and the Netherlands all made complaints concerning violations of eight articles of the European Convention on Human Rights, and before long Greece left the Council of Europe before they could be removed. They were then expelled from the European Economic Community (the European

---

[1] (Papaeti, 2013, p. 2)

common market and a precursor to the EU), which cost the Greek economy dearly.

At the time, during the Cold War, and especially considering the Ancient Greeks were considered to have invented democracy, it was a constant source of embarrassment to the west to have a country in the Western Bloc seen to be constantly and flagrantly violating the human rights of its own citizens. Despite that, the west continued to support the military junta in Greece in the name of the Cold War. President Bill Clinton, much later in 1999, would apologise to the Greeks for this on behalf of the USA, telling them "When the junta took over in 1967, the United States allowed its interests in prosecuting the Cold War to prevail over its interest, I should say its obligation, to support democracy, which was, after all, the cause for which we fought the Cold War"[1].

The Junta's relationship with Makarios

The Greek Junta had a difficult relationship with Makarios. Makarios was a royalist, loyal to the king of Greece, who himself was an opponent of the Junta. In December 1967 the king had tried to seize power from

---

[1] (BBC News, 1999)

the junta using the naval and air forces still loyal to him. His coup failed and he was exiled to Rome. Shortly after, Makarios sent a telegram to the king, which was also published in a press release, wishing him an "early return to his throne for the good of the Greek Nation"[1].

The junta were keen on enosis, and even offered Turkey a military base on the island if they'd agree to it. Makarios started to distance himself from enosis in response, not wanting to be associated with the Greek regime. In 1968, Makarios ran for re-election for president as a pro-independence (rather than pro-enosis) candidate, and won the vote with 95% of the Greek Cypriot vote.[2]

Grivas was still staunchly supportive of Greece and, as head of the Greek Cypriot military, was heavily backed by Greek soldiers and weapons. Makarios would come to regret his decision to invite Grivas back to lead the military in 1964, becoming increasingly frightened that Grivas and his men would overthrow him at any time on the whims of the new regime in Greece.

---

[1] (Kiralp, 2014, p. 162)
[2] (Kiralp, 2014)

THE 1967 CRISIS

In the winter of 1967, three years after his return, Grivas announced his presence on the island in a characteristically bloody and violent fashion.

First of all, an influential and charismatic leader of the Turkish Cypriot community, Rauf Denktaş, was arrested by the Greek Cypriot police force. Denktaş was a protégé and friend of Dr. Fazıl Küçük and at the time, was an important figure in the Turkish Cypriot resistance. Much later in the 1973 elections, he succeeded his friend as the Turkish Cypriot leader when Dr. Küçük was forced to retire by ill health.

Rauf Denktaş
Turkish Republic of Northern Cyprus President's Office

Denktaş was quickly released by the Greek Cypriot police force as there was no admissible evidence against him.[1] At the same time, the Greek Cypriot

---

[1] (Mirbagheri, 1998, p. 62)

National Guard, led by Grivas, executed planned attacks on two Turkish Cypriot villages.

Since July 1967, the UN had strongly advised Greek Cypriots stop patrolling in the Turkish Cypriot enclave of Ayios Theodhoros, due to tensions between the Greeks and Turks. Negotiations were ongoing regarding the resumption of these Greek patrols, and the UN, Turkey and the Turkish Cypriot leadership all looked close to agreeing to their non-violent return. Despite this the Greeks sent heavily armed soldiers to patrol the village just prior to the conclusion of peace talks in a planned, and deliberately provocative, show of force.

The Chief of Staff of the UNFICYP described the actions in the Ayios Theodhoros in the following way:

> "*There seems little doubt that General Grivas was determined to provoke the Turks into a fight, for even UN Special Representative Osorio-Tafall and UNFICYP Commander Martola were making strong representations to the 'government' to stop this provocative action, Grivas ordered yet another patrol into the village in the early afternoon of the 15th*"[1]

---

[1] (Coşkun, 2015, p. 44)

The Turkish Cypriots fought back and were beaten easily by the heavily armed Greek forces, and the Greeks took control of the enclave after just a few hours of fighting.

At the same time, the Cypriot Defence Council (led by Makarios) and the Greek Junta had arranged a separate military campaign in another Turkish village – Kophinou – in a coordinated attack on the Turkish enclaves of Cyprus. Grivas and the Cypriot National Guard attacked Kophinou on 15th November 1967. They used mortars and armoured vehicles and, of course, suffered no casualties or serious injuries themselves. The mortars did however cause significant Turkish Cypriot casualties. The Greek Cypriot press jubilantly celebrated the death of 22 Turkish Cypriots, labelling them "terrorists". The Turkish Cypriot newspaper Halkin Sesi, in contrast, spoke of 100 Turkish Cypriot casualties; including an 80 year old man who was burned and killed by the Greek troops, as well as unarmed civilians who were murdered by heavily armed Greek soldiers.[1]

The Greek Cypriot state saw the operations in Kophinou and Ayios Theodhoros as a great success

---

[1] (Kiralp, 2014, p. 160)

and celebrated them with maximum press publicity. If the Greek Cypriot state had kept a lower profile over these violent operations against Turkish Cypriot enclaves, it has been said that they may have quietly gotten away with them.[1]

The Turkish response to November 1967

On the 16th November, the day after the attacks, the Turkish government gathered in Ankara and immediately warned Makarios and the Greek government that the Turkish Air Force would begin a bombing campaign in Cyprus if the Greek Cypriot army continued to occupy Kophinou and Ayios Theodhoros. Greece agreed to order Grivas to withdraw his forces immediately.

The British Foreign and Commonwealth Office's Research Department described "an attack led by General Grivas, who had returned to Cyprus in 1964 and become commander of the Defence of Cyprus, on the Turkish inhabitants of two villages and their houses. Over 20 Turkish-Cypriots were killed. Ankara's reaction was immediate. If the Greek and Greek Cypriots' forces had not been withdrawn (from

---

[1] (Mirbagheri, 1998, p. 62)

the occupied villages) by dawn the next day, Turkish bombers would have gone to action"[1].

The Turkish Cypriot leader Dr. Fazıl Küçük was still not happy and sent a telegram to Turkish Prime Minister Suleyman Demirel asking for Turkish military intervention in Cyprus, and Turkish parliament did indeed pass a law authorising the government to intervene militarily in Cyprus if it became necessary. Indeed the British ambassador to Ankara noted himself that Turkey were ready to invade to protect the Turkish Cypriots, describing them as "ready to go"[2].

The general public and opposition parties in Turkey sympathised strongly with the Turkish Cypriots too, especially after the murders in Kophinou and the massacres in 1963, and the Turkish government were under a lot of pressure domestically to do more to help in Cyprus.

In response to this pressure, Turkey ordered the Greeks to allow freedom of movement for Turkish Cypriots, and more importantly demanded that Grivas himself leave Cyprus and return to Greece. They also demanded any Greek forces in excess of the numbers

---

[1] (Coşkun, 2015, p. 47)
[2] (Coşkun, 2015, p. 48)

allowed in the agreements of 1960 leave the island immediately[1] (there were somewhere between 10,000 and 20,000 troops from Greece on the island despite the Treaty of Alliance allowing for only 950). The British prime minister sent a message to Makarios urging him to accept the Turkish proposals. In a way, these repercussions worked well for Makarios, who would have had more autonomy without the Greek Junta's presence on the island, and he duly accepted.

Given the brutal treatment of the Turkish Cypriots, Turks felt that the Turkish government still hadn't done enough and there were pointed criticisms of the government in the Turkish Grand National Assembly, including even calls for a vote of no confidence in the Demirel government. The Turkish response also disappointed the Turkish Cypriots themselves, who were desperate for a permanent solution to the Cyprus problem. The British Foreign and Commonwealth Office noted that if the island were to see anything like the events of 1967 again, it would "be difficult for a government in Turkey to remain in power without sending the Turkish troops into action"[2].

---

[1] (Mirbagheri, 1998, p. 63)
[2] (Coşkun, 2015, pp. 55-58)

THE RISE OF EOKA B

From 1968, thanks to what the British Foreign Office called "the evacuation of the 'illegal' Greek troops who were in Cyprus and a sharp reduction in Greek involvement in the problem"[1], tensions between Greek Cypriots and Turkish Cypriots started to ease and their friendship started to show signs of returning. This was in sharp contrast to the years before 1967, where the Turks and Greeks lived separately and tensely in neighbouring villages, changing local street names, village names and town names, and celebrating different holidays, according to the ethnic group which controlled the area. The economy had been booming, and whereas previously it had only been the Greek Cypriots who had benefited whilst the Turks lived in heavily patrolled slum enclaves, both communities could now enjoy the products of the country's success.

The Turkish Cypriots continued to live in enclaves after the evacuation of Greek troops, but now with the same freedom of movement the Greek Cypriots had

---

[1] (Coşkun, 2015, p. 54)

enjoyed, working and trading with the Greek Cypriots[1], and interacting once again as old friends.

Grivas returns to the island again

In 1971, with backing from Greece, George Grivas snuck back to Cyprus in secret to form EOKA-B. Grivas was a hardline enosisist, a Greek nationalist, and – worried that Makarios had won the most recent democratic elections with a huge landslide on a pro-independence ticket – wanted to fight what he felt was Makarios's unacceptable compromise.

He joined forces with the National Front, a terrorist organisation which shared his aims of either forcing Makarios to toe the pro-enosis line or resigning from his position. The National Front had already made an attempt on Makarios's life in 1970 with the help of an inside man - Cypriot Minister of Interior Polycarpos Georgadjis. Georgadjis had been killed attempting to flee the country shortly after his involvement had become known. A confidential telegram written by the British High Commissioner to Cyprus to the Foreign and Commonwealth Office suggested that Turkey had reliable information that Brigadier Dimitrios Ioannidis

---

[1] (Papadakis, Locating the Cyprus Problem: Ethnic Conflict and the Politics of Space, 2005, p. 85)

– the head of Greek Military Police, and a member of the Greek Junta – was the mastermind behind the assassination attempt on Makarios, and that a Greek officer in the Cypriot Army had been ordered to murder Georgadjis in an attempt to silence him. The National Front had also been carrying out attacks on Cypriot police headquarters, local government offices, and stealing arms and ammunition from the Cypriot administration. [1]

Makarios responded to these dangers by importing a large quantity of arms and ammunition – including bazookas, rifles, and mortars – to arm his own supporters with in an attempt to protect himself from Grivas and EOKA B. The Greek Junta requested that Makarios hand these weapons over the UN, and when he refused they demanded that he resign, even offering to recall Grivas to Greece again if he did. Around this time the British ambassador to Greece sent a telegram to the British Foreign and Commonweath Office, expressing his fear of a civil war between Greek Cypriot Makarios and Greek Cypriot Grivas supporters.[2] In March 1972, in order to lessen the tensions, the

---

[1] (Kiralp, 2014, pp. 146-177)
[2] (Kiralp, 2014, pp. 146-177)

UNFICYP effectively confiscated these weapons, keeping them locked in UNFICYP policed camps.[1]

Makarios also sent Glafcos Clerides (a senior member of his party, a fellow EOKA member, and later president of Cyprus) to the USA to beg for help against the Greek Junta. In return the Americans sent a US ambassador to Greece, and successfully convinced the leader of the Junta and dictator of Greece at the time – Georgios Papadopoulos – to allow Makarios to continue his reign peacefully.

EOKA B continued their campaign however, in 1973 even kidnapping the Cypriot Minister of Justice and sending a letter to Makarios asking him to resign. Makarios publicly branded Grivas "insane", and (ironically considering their history as comrades in EOKA together) called upon Grivas to abandon terrorism and use democratic methods to propagate his ideology instead.[2] In the meantime, Makarios was again voted president. He was the only candidate.

While EOKA enjoyed broad support from the Greek Cypriot population in the 1950s, EOKA B did not garner anywhere near the same levels of support. They

---

[1] (The United Nations, 2020)
[2] (Kiralp, 2014, p. 181)

were branded a terrorist organisation internationally, and even Makarios himself – a founding member of the original EOKA group – branded EOKA B a terrorist organisation, accusing them of being directed by Athens in a speech to the UN Security Council.[1] He accused the Greek government of trying to abolish the state of Cyprus with their support of the organisation.[2]

---

[1] (Makarios, 1974)
[2] (Lieberman, 2013, p. 266)

THE TURKISH INTERVENTION OF 1974

There were two events that served as a catalyst for further trouble on the island. The first was Brigadier Dimitris Ioannidis – one of the officers who had helped to plan and execute the Greek Junta coup – overthrowing the Junta leader Papadopoulos, who he believed had become weak, and taking charge himself in November 1973. Ioannidis was described by Time Magazine as a "a rigid, puritanical xenophobe"[1] and by the Daily Telegraph as the "brutal head" of the military police at whose headquarters "opponents of the regime, both civilian and military, were systematically tortured"[2]. The second event, two months later in January 1974, was the death of George Grivas – a man who had been both a powerful ally of Makarios as leader of EOKA, and a powerful enemy as leader of EOKA B. He died of heart failure while hiding out in a house in Cyprus and, despite their recent differences, Makarios declared three days of national mourning for him.

---

[1] (Davison, 2010)
[2] (The Telegraph, 2010)

A Greek coup d'etat in Cyprus

In July 1974, with Makarios becoming increasingly annoyed with the Greek Junta's involvement in Cyprus, he wrote an open public letter to Athens in which he noted that "The National Guard, which is staffed and controlled by the Greek officers, has been from the outset the main supplier of men and material to EOKA B". Makarios noted that it was an "undeniable reality" that Greek officers were supporting the "unlawful and nationally harmful" EOKA B telling the president that "the root of the evil is very deep, reaching as far as Athens". He even went as far as to tell the Greek dictator directly: "I cannot say that I have a special liking for military regimes, particularly in Greece"[1]. Later that week Cypriot police loyal to Makarios arrested a high ranking EOKA B officer, and discovered a stash of EOKA B documents outlining the future plans of the organisation in his possession. The documents infuriated Makarios even more, leading him to drastically reduce the strength of the National Guard, sending around 600 officers and soldiers back to Greece. While announcing this reduction Makarios also asked publicly "whether the Greek Government will give orders for the dissolution of EOKA B, the

---

[1] (Kiralp, 2014, p. 233)

terrorist organisation which has led the Greek Cypriots to the brink of civil war and which is supported and maintained by cadres of the Greek military regime"[1] and angrily reiterated his accusation that the Junta were causing trouble in an attempt to end the state of Cyprus and unite the island with Greece.

Days later, the National Guard, supported by Greek military colonels, attacked the Presidential Palace with tanks and armoured vehicles. Makarios managed to flee the palace, but the Cyprus Broadcasting Corporation radio station was captured by Greece, who announced to the nation that Makarios had died and the National Guard were now in charge. Makarios, from a hiding place on the island, also broadcasted a message to the Greek Cypriot people, asking them to resist the Junta's new government in Cyprus. Around 500 people were killed in the ensuing conflict, the majority being policemen or Greek Cypriot civilians who had resisted the Junta dictatorship, with another 1000 people arrested by the new administration.[2]

Makarios managed to flee to London, where he was told by the British prime minister that they still considered him to be the legal head of state. The

---

[1] (Kiralp, 2014, p. 235)
[2] (Kiralp, 2014, p. 238)

Turkish prime minister Ecevit also visited the British prime minister to inform him that Turkey and the UK were obliged by the treaties of 1960 to restore constitutional order in Cyprus. Both Makarios and Turkey were told by the British that, despite being named a guarantor power of Cyprus by the Treaty of Guarantee, they had no intention to help or intervene. The Junta were convinced that Turkey would be dissuaded from intervening without US or UK backing, as they had been in 1964.[1]

The Turkish victory over the Junta

Greece put Nikos Sampson in charge of Cyprus after the coup. Sampson had been a prominent EOKA and EOKA B fighter, would carry out executions for EOKA, and had been elected to the Cyprus House of Representatives in 1969 on the slogan "Death to Turks". He had achieved infamy after leading vicious attacks on Turkish Cypriot civilians during the events of Bloody Christmas in 1963 and 1964, and had been affectionately nicknamed the "Butcher of Omorphita" for his brutality in the Turkish quarter. Denktaş

---

[1] (Oberling, 1982, p. 163)

described Sampson's appointment as "as unacceptable as Adolf Hitler would be as President of Israel".[1]

Sampson's new position was part of the reason Denktaş – leader of the Turkish Cypriot community – was worried enough to contact Turkey: "I felt anxious because Nicos Sampson, who came into power, was insane and he was a murderer. As soon as I heard about the coup, I expressed to my people that it was an intra-Hellenic issue and asked them to not to get involved. I immediately contacted Ankara and I asked Turkey to take action."[2] Denktaş believed that, now that Greece had successfully taken Cyprus and overthrown the Greek Cypriot government, this was the last chance for Turkey to reverse enosis and save the Turkish Cypriot people from certain death.

On the 20th July, five days after the Greek invasion of the island, Turkey launched its first military intervention in Cyprus, in accordance with Article IV of the Treaty of Guarantee. The Turks landed 25,000 soldiers on the island, taking 7% of the island under its possession. The Turkish military easily managed to reach and safeguard the Turkish Cypriot enclave in Nicosia, where they negotiated a ceasefire and begun

---

[1] (Oberling, 1982, p. 160)
[2] (Kiralp, 2014, p. 244)

peace talks. Sampson later declared that if Turkey had not intervened "I would not only have proclaimed ENOSIS (union between Cyprus and Greece), I would have annihilated the Turks in Cyprus"[1].

In the aftermath of Turkey's intervention, Ioannidis lost the support of senior officers in the Greek military. There was anger and disappointment after the failure to successfully invade Cyprus, and the loss of support for the Junta lead to the collapse of the military dictatorship in Greece as the army itself decided to hand power back to the democratic government.[2] In the 3 days following the Turkish intervention in Cyprus, Constantine Karamanlis – the Greek Prime Minister prior to the Junta – returned from exile and became Greek Prime Minister again, restoring democracy in Greece. The collapse of the Junta meant Sampson was also forced to resign from his position in Cyprus, and eventually Makarios returned to office.

What came to be known as "Greece's Nuremberg trials"[3] came shortly after. The men responsible for the original coup in Greece (including Georgios Papadopoulos and Dimitrios Ioannidis) were put on trial for their crimes – high treason, torture, mutiny,

---

[1] (Halil, 2019)
[2] (Haralambous, 2017, p. 308)
[3] (Halil, 2019)

91

and other crimes. They were sentenced to spend the rest of their lives in prison. Nikos Sampson was also sentenced to 20 years in prison for abuse of power for his involvement in the Cypriot coup.

The second Turkish intervention

After the first Turkish intervention, peace talks begun between Denktaş, the Greek Cypriots, and the three guarantor states – Greece, Turkey, and Britain. Turkey and Denktaş demanded a bi-zonal federation, as it seemed to them the only way to keep the Turkish Cypriot community safe from the attacks they'd been subjected to over the decades. Makarios refused, claiming that a bi-zonal federation was "unacceptable"[1].

The Turks felt Greece were trying to buy time, and after calling on the UN to "stop the genocide of Turkish Cypriots" and emphasising that they "will not allow Turkish Cypriots to be massacred"[2], they executed the second phase of what they described as the Turkish Peace Operation. The supremacy of the Turkish army was enough, according to the US Foreign Secretary

---

[1] (Kiralp, 2014, p. 243)
[2] (Halil, 2019)

Henry Kissinger[1], that they have could taken the whole of the small island – which was just off their coastline – in a few days. This worried the UK and US, as they had military bases on the island.

On the same day that Turkey launched its military intervention, Greek Cypriot EOKA B fighters invaded Turkish Cypriot villages and carried out bloody rapes and murders of the Turkish Cypriot civilians living there[2], in a last-ditch attempt to ethnically cleanse the Turks from the island.

The Greek Cypriot militia entered the village coffeehouses in Maratha, Santalaris and Aloda, arrested all Turkish Cypriot men of fighting age and took them away as prisoners of war. They then raped the women, girls and boys, before killing all of the remaining witnesses in the village. A tiny number of Turkish Cypriots managed to escape (only three people were able to escape from the massacre in Aloda[3]) while the rest were buried in unmarked mass graves. The UN described these massacres as a "crime against humanity". In the village of Tochni, EOKA B men and officers of the Greek Army arrested all of the Turkish Cypriot men and boys, kept them overnight, and then

---

[1] (Bora, 2013, p. 40)
[2] (Christofides, 2016, p. 11)
[3] (Oberling, 1982, p. 185)

in the morning executed them all with automatic machine guns before burying them too in mass graves. The Turkish Cypriot inhabitants of a number of villages across the island were "almost entirely wiped out."[1] In the Turkish Cypriot quarter of Paphos, a three-year-old boy was found by a UN observer with 30 to 40 bullet holes in his body.[2]

In January 1964, 21 Turkish Cypriots were found buried. A British investigation found that they had been patients at the Nicosia General Hospital that had had their throats slit by medical staff.[3] The Greek Cypriot authorities disputed this version of events, and contested that the bodies had only had to be buried quickly because that the Turkish Cypriot leadership had refused to do so themselves. Some of the bodies were still tied up when they were discovered.[4]

In some areas, such as Larnaca and Limassol, where Turkish Cypriots had surrendered, thousands were taken to prisons and makeshift concentration camps in schools and football stadiums where they

---

[1] (Campbell-Thomson, 2014, p. 68)
[2] (Oberling, 1982, p. 186)
[3] (Safty A. , 2011, p. 349)
[4] (Richmond & Ker-Lindsay, 2001, p. 201)

were left to sleep on bare concrete floors with little food and no medical attention.[1]

The Turkish army did eventually arrive, to the great relief of the surviving Turkish Cypriots, and took 36% of the island[2], stopping after they'd successfully occupied the Turkish quarter of Nicosia. Thereafter, many Greek Cypriots either fled, or were pressured by Turkish Cypriots, to the south of the island. Turkish Cypriots in the southern part of the island snuck to the northern half of the island in the middle of night, making sure to stay in the darkness, trying to avoid Greek Cypriot patrols looking to block them from moving to safety. Turkish Cypriots caught trying to sneak to the north were captured and beaten by Greek Cypriot police.[3]

The Turkish interventions brought relative peace to the island, and there have been no major violent incidents in the almost five decades since.[4] By the end of the conflict however, a third of Cypriots had become displaced from their original homes, many had died, and thousands had fled the island completely.[5]

---

[1] (Oberling, 1982, p. 172)
[2] (Kiralp, 2014, p. 243)
[3] (Oberling, 1982, p. 5 intro)
[4] (Bora, 2013, p. 41)
5 (Global IDP Project, 2005)

The immediate aftermath

After the events of 1974, UN-brokered peace talks begun in the neutral setting of Vienna and the Greek Cypriot administration reluctantly agreed that any future settlement would be based on a bi-zonal federation whereby the Turkish Cypriots would be free to govern themselves in their own territory.[1]

The Turkish Cypriot administration in the north formed the Turkish Federated State of Cyprus – a first step towards what the Turkish Cypriots hoped would be a federated Cypriot state, whereby both communities could govern themselves autonomously, in separate states, but under one country. Denktaş hoped that the Greek Cypriot government would see themselves as equal to the Turkish Cypriots, and also proclaim their own federated state. The Greek Cypriots were unhappy with the Turkish Cypriots taking actions that hadn't been covered or agreed in the peace talks, and took it to the UN, who expressed regret at the unilateral actions of the Turkish Cypriots in UN security council resolution 367[2] and declared their

---

[1] (Ker-Lindsay J. , 2017)
[2] (UN Security Council, 1975)

worry that it might compromise the ongoing negotiations.

The peace talks also brought about the Voluntary Exchange of Populations agreement. The agreement was signed in Vienna on the 2nd August 1975 and allowed for any Greek Cypriots in the north to move south and any Turkish Cypriots in the south to move north with the assistance of the UN.[1] For the first time in years, Cypriot citizens could now live in safety.

---

[1] (Campbell-Thomson, 2014, p. 69)

THE FORMATION OF THE TRNC

Unfortunately, little else was achieved in the peace talks in Vienna. The UN, as they had since Bloody Christmas in 1963, continued only to recognise the Greek Cypriot administration as the legitimate representatives of the Republic of Cyprus. This meant that while Greek Cypriot representatives were able to address the UN General Assembly, Turkish Cypriots were excluded almost entirely from the debate. The Greek Cypriot administration helped this along with an aggressive and effective campaign to assert that it was the sole rightful government on the island.[1]

This all came to a head in 1983 when, on 13th May, and despite concerns from the British government, the UN General Assembly passed Resolution 37/253. The resolution stressed the Assembly's belief that the Greek Cypriot government had a territorial right to the whole island as well as a right to govern everyone on the island, and called "upon all States to support and

---

[1] (Campbell-Thomson, 2014, p. 72)

help the Government of Cyprus" to exercise those rights.

To the Turkish Cypriot state, the United Nations calling for support for an administration which they firmly believed had surely lost its legitimacy after violating the founding constitution of the country – imposing economic and physical blockades, banishing from government, and carrying out brutal armed attacks on a constitutionally protected Muslim minority – was infuriating, and Denktaş announced, in response, his intention to declare an independent Turkish Cypriot state.[1]

A unilateral declaration of independence

To gain international recognition when declaring independence, a country has to first gain the support of the world's most powerful countries. The only country to have ever declared its independence unilaterally and gained UN recognition was Bangladesh in 1972 – who done so after securing support from all five permanent members of the UN Security Council – Britain, China, France, Russia and the United States.

---

[1] (Campbell-Thomson, 2014, p. 73)

With regards to Cyprus however, the British government made it clear immediately that they wished to avoid a Turkish Cypriot unilateral declaration of independence (UDI). The British foreign office noted that a UDI would harm ongoing UN talks, and was contrary to the 1960 treaties. Britain also noted their previous experience with UDIs in Rhodesia and indicated that they were keen to avoid a repeat. Practical implications were also considered by the British foreign office, including the potential reduction of influence Britain may have over a militarily important island for them. The United States, who also benefit from British military bases on the island, assisted by putting pressure on Turkey to restrain the Turkish Cypriot administration.[1]

The western powers were also worried about the wider repercussions of a UDI. They were worried about the precedent it would set, tensions it would cause between Turkey and Greece in NATO, and especially worried about what they considered to be the 'extreme' socialist Greek government pulling Greece out of NATO if they were unhappy with the situation and the international response to it.[2]

---

[1] (Ker-Lindsay J. , 2017, p. 4)
[2] (Ker-Lindsay J. , 2017, p. 6)

When Britain informed the Turkish government that there would be no question of British recognition of a new Turkish Cypriot state, Turkey warned Denktaş against a UDI, but also warned Britain against believing that the Turkish Cypriot government would and could only act with Ankara's permission.[1]

Serious concern started to mount that Denktaş might make good on his threats and that there may be little London or indeed Ankara could do about it, and while the British High Commissioner in Nicosia informed Denktaş that the British government "understood and even sympathised"[2] with Turkish Cypriot concerns over the actions of the UN, they also made plans for their response in case a UDI did come to pass. It was noted that there was huge domestic support in North Cyprus for a safe independent country for Turkish Cypriots, and that the credibility of the Turkish Cypriot government might be affected if they failed to make good on their threats to declare independence.[3]

On the 15th November 1983, the Turkish Republic of North Cyprus, a semi-presidential secular democratic republic, was proclaimed. The declaration

[1] (Ker-Lindsay J. , 2017, p. 4)
[2] (Ker-Lindsay J. , 2017, p. 4)
[3] (Ker-Lindsay J. , 2017, p. 5)

of independence was passed through parliament unanimously and emphasised that North Cyprus "firmly adhered to the view that the two peoples of Cyprus were destined to co-exist side by side and could and should find a peaceful, just and durable solution through negotiations on the basis of equality",[1] reaffirming the Turkish Cypriots wishes to re-establish a partnership on the island through further negotiations, but on a more equal footing.

The international response

The British government immediately began to lead efforts within the UN to condemn the move. In a particularly telling comment, the British permanent representative at the UN mused that Britain may be able to "gain good marks"[2] with the Greeks by coming out strongly against the Turkish Cypriots, as well as being able to get out ahead of the Greeks and avoid "unwelcome" elements that the Greeks might demand if they were to lead efforts, such as sanctions against Turkey.

---

[1] (TRNC Ministry of Foreign Affairs, 2020)
[2] (Ker-Lindsay J. , 2017, p. 7)

These British efforts lead to UN Security Council Resolution 541, which declared the TRNC to be illegal and called on all states not to recognise it.

THE GREEK CYPRIOT REACTION

The Greek Cypriot administered Republic of Cyprus had already managed to maintain the sympathy of the international community, in spite of everything, with the help of effective and aggressive international lobbying. They were successfully able to maintain United Nations recognition as the sole legitimate government of the island throughout the rule of the foreign Greek Junta, the fundamental unilateral changes to the constitution, the creation of the Turkish Cypriot slums in the 1960s, and the attempted genocide of the Turkish Cypriot community. The declaration of the TRNC in 1983, and the British-led UN condemnation of that declaration, had handed the Greek Cypriot administration yet another huge win internationally.

A new shared narrative

In 1975 – on the first anniversary of the Greek coup in Cyprus – a key debate took place in the Greek Cypriot House of Representatives regarding the country's return to democracy. It was clearly understood at the time[1], both domestically and internationally, that the Greek Cypriot administration had not only failed to fulfil enosis, but had failed to prevent (and in fact, had caused or helped to cause) both the Greek dictatorship-led coup and the formation of the Turkish state in North Cyprus. Trust in the Greek Cypriot government had eroded and would have to be restored.

All parties in parliament that day in 1975 came to the consensus that, to preserve and rebuild a democratic Republic of Cyprus, they must do two things. As political scientist Dr. Iosif Kovras reports: "All speakers insisted on the twin pillars of this 'invented unity': the need for unity and reconciliation, coupled with respect for the institutions of the Republic."[2]

In order to achieve this, all members of parliament and party leaders agreed to a common reading of recent history in order to, as future president of the Republic of Cyprus Glafcos Clerides described it, "fulfil a common struggle for the survival of Cyprus". The leader of the communist party AKEL, the most popular

---

[1] (Kovras, 2014, p. 52)
[2] (Kovras, 2014, p. 52)

political party in Cyprus at the time, stressed the need to "keep the flag of patriotic unity high".

Political scientist Dr. Kovras notes that to help overcome divisions and create unity, the Greek Cypriot political elite, by determining "what would be remembered and what would be silenced"[1] created a "widely shared version of the past" as part of a strategy to accentuate a Greek Cypriot "culture of victimhood".[2] He posits that "*selective memory*, or selective oblivion, became the founding tenet of the pact that facilitated the transition to peace and democracy in the RoC after 1974".[3]

In modern times, the level of trust domestically in the Greek Cypriot state institutions is "remarkably high", and challenges to the state narrative remain hugely unlikely, even when proof has been uncovered which casts doubt over official versions of events.[4]

Missing persons

An example of this political framing is the missing persons issue. The Greek Cypriot administration has

---

[1] (Kovras, 2014, p. 49)
[2] (Kovras, 2014, p. 52)
[3] (Kovras, 2014, p. 51)
[4] (Kovras, 2014, p. 54)

claimed to have 1,619 missing persons, which they blame solely and fully on the state of Turkey. There have been 12 resolutions, all passed unanimously in the House of Representatives, that identify Turkey as solely responsible for these missing people.

The first peculiar thing about this issue is the definition the Greek Cypriot political classes decided to use to determine a 'missing person'. The state defines a missing person as a "Greek-Cypriot who is still missing since July 20th 1974, due to the Turkish invasion... and the state has no positive information s/he died", consciously deciding to create a casual link between missing people and the date of the Turkish operations of 1974. The definition also purposefully excludes Turkish Cypriots, many of whom went missing as a result of Greek Cypriot paramilitary violence in the 1960s and early 1970s, despite them also being Republic of Cyprus citizens.[1] The conscious framing of missing Greek Cypriots as a Turkish problem in the state definition also purposefully overlooks the huge number of Greek Cypriot civilians who went missing at the hands of the EOKA paramilitaries and the Greek Junta prior to 1974.[2]

---

[1] (Kovras, 2014, p. 51)
[2] (Kovras, 2014, p. 51)

The other peculiar thing about this narrative is the unconventional method by which the Greek Cypriot administration reached the number 1,619. Until 1980, the number of missing was claimed to be around 2,000. In 1980, when it seemed like the original list of 2,000 might have included duplicate entries, a Greek Cypriot missing persons committee provided the UN with a list of 1,510 names. This new list also contained duplicate entries. Details around the disappearance were only given for 425 of the names on the list, and hundreds on the list had no identity card numbers. Details in many cases on the list were said to be "very vague"[1]. In 1981, for the first time, the Greek Cypriot government started to use the number 1,619. The government refused to indicate to international organisations and journalists how they reached this new number, but there have been a number of lists all with different sets of names.[2] The Republic of Cyprus government has never released an official list.

In fact, many of the "missing persons" on the Greek Cypriot list were eventually discovered buried in areas controlled by the Greek Cypriot state.[3] In spite of this, many Greek Cypriot politicians remained loyal to the

---

[1] (Cassia, 2005, p. 51)
[2] (Cassia, 2005, p. 51)
[3] (Kovras, 2014, p. 115)

narrative of the 1,619 missing, and journalists who helped to uncover mistruths from the state about these missing people received death threats from Greek nationalists.[1]

The Greek Cypriot political elite have used this number – 1,619 – consistently and repeatedly in internationally oriented efforts to expel the Turks from Cyprus.[2] The tactic has been effective in attracting sympathy internationally but has done very little for the relatives of any genuinely missing Cypriots.[3]

In 2001, the European Court of Human Rights found definitively that "there was no proof that any of the missing persons were killed in circumstances for which [Turkey] could be held responsible; nor did the Commission find any evidence to the effect that any of the persons taken into custody were still being detained or kept in servitude by the [Turkish] State."[4]

Occupied land

Another complaint of the Greek Cypriot state is the idea that the Turkish army have 'invaded' and are

---

[1] (Kovras, 2014, p. 54)
[2] (Cassia, 2005, p. 74)
[3] (Kovras, 2014, p. 53)
[4] (European Court of Human Rights, 2001)

'occupying' land that they feel should belong to the Republic of Cyprus. "Cyprus is Greek" is a frequently uttered statement.[1]

In 2001, the European Court of Human Rights partly sided with the Greek Cypriot state on this, ruling that the border between TRNC and the Republic of Cyprus was in violation of the human right to property, concluding that Greek Cypriots should be entitled to return to any home or property they may have owned in the north prior to 1974.[2]

Turkish Cypriots who were forced out of their homes in the southern half of the island were left unmentioned in the judgement. The Voluntary Exchange of Population agreement, an agreement that the UN helped to broker and execute with the idea that they would make sure each migration was completely voluntary, was also left unmentioned.

Turkish settlers

There have also been concerns, from both the Turkish Cypriot and the Greek Cypriot communities, about the number of Turkish settlers that now live in

---

[1] (Diez, 2001, p. 40)
[2] (European Court of Human Rights, 2001, p. 44)

the TRNC. Mainland Turks were initially encouraged to northern Cyprus to replace Greek Cypriot manpower in the agricultural sector. In the Republic of Cyprus, westerners can be surprised to hear the vitriol now directed at Turks, and specifically at Turkish immigrants from the mainland. Professor of Political Science, Adrienne Christiansen recalls:

> *"Pejorative and inflammatory statements against this population frequently are printed in the Greek Cypriot press. Turkish immigrants commonly are described in newspaper reports or during informal conversation as dark, dirty, black beards, peasants, squatters, interlopers, illegal occupiers, criminals, rapists, thieves, drug-dealers, uneducated, poor, unclean, lazy, religious, gypsies, or even 'Anatolian apes.' Anti-immigrant sentiment was everywhere when I lived on the island during the fall of 2003. Even the words 'settler,' 'Turk,' and 'Muslim' served as vicious epithets."[1]*

Signs outside Greek Cypriot airports greet arrivals with the words "WE DEMAND ALL TURKISH TROOPS AND SETTLERS LEAVE CYPRUS". The denigration of Turkish immigrants by Greek Cypriots is perhaps unsurprising, but the Turkish Cypriot view of these settlers is more interesting.

---

[1] (Christiansen, 2005)

The settlers have historically been relatively poor and from rural areas of Turkey, and there are significant cultural differences in dress, language and religious practices, between the majority of Turkish settlers in Cyprus and the majority of native-born Turkish Cypriots.[1] Migrants from mainland Turkey typically work for a much lower average wage, putting downward pressure on already low salaries, and are generally much more religious than the relatively non-religious native population. There are worries within the proudly secular Turkish Cypriot community that, under Erdoğan, Turkey might push more religious practices on to the island's population,[2] and the more religious makeup of settlers from rural Turkey can perhaps serve to play in to these fears.

Former TRNC president Mustafa Akıncı distanced himself from Ankara throughout his time in office from 2015 to 2020 in an attempt to assuage some of these worries. He criticised Ankara's foreign policy publicly, and declared the need for "independent, brotherly relations" with Turkey. He stressed the need for the Turkish Cypriots to keep their distinct "secular, democratic, and plural" identity, and had a fairly tense

---

[1] (Christiansen, 2005)
[2] (Politico, 2019)

relationship with the Turkish administration as a result.[1] He restarted negotiations directly with the Greek Cypriot president soon after taking office, with the view to reunifying the island and cutting the dependence on Turkey. These talks would eventually collapse without a deal in 2017 after Greek Cypriot MPs – mostly from the ultranationalist National Popular Front party – voted to commemorate the Greek Orthodox referendum ran by Archbishop Makarios in 1950 with 'Enosis Day' celebrations, calling for all secondary school pupils to learn about the ideals behind enosis despite fierce TRNC opposition.[2]

Akıncı lost re-election to Ersin Tatar in 2020, gaining 48% of the vote in the run-off compared to Tatar's 52%. Tatar ran with the support of Turkey and campaigned on a platform for closer relations with Ankara. While many were happy after Tatar's win, thousands of Akıncı supporters – including many major politicians and indeed Akıncı himself – attended protests shortly after the result, chanting slogans like "Ankara, keep your hands off us"[3]

[1] (The Guardian, 2020)
[2] (Al Jazeera, 2017)
[3] (Cyprus Mail, 2020)

WHAT'S HAPPENED SINCE?

Northern Cyprus is an observer state of ECO (Economic Cooperation Organization founded by Iran, Pakistan and Turkey), and of the OIC (Organisation of Islamic Cooperation) under the title "Turkish Cypriot State", and also of PACE (Parliamentary Assembly of the Council of Europe) under the title "Turkish Cypriot Community".

Aside from that, recognition of the TRNC has been almost non-existent. Turkey is the only nation to officially recognise the state. Pakistan and Bangladesh recognised the country briefly, but quickly changed their mind after pressure from the UN, Greece and the Republic of Cyprus. Severe international embargoes supported by the UN, the EU and the Greek Cypriot state exist against almost every part of TRNC's economy and culture. They can't fly internationally, send post, export goods, play international sports, their food certificates were deemed unacceptable by the European Union, even concerts have been blocked and cancelled after extensive pressure from the Greek Cypriot administration.[1]

In contrast, the Greek Cypriot governed Republic of Cyprus is a member of the EU and the UN, and is a high-income country with an economy built on a strong foundation of tourism and finance, operating as an international centre of tax avoidance for wealthier countries.

Mass migration

The economic situation in TRNC, and the decades of oppression and violence that preceded the Turkish interventions of 1974, has unfortunately meant that the majority of Turkish Cypriots have migrated away from the island. A substantial number of Greek Cypriots also left during the troubles.

Citizens of Cyprus had been given British passports when the island was annexed in to the empire in the 1940s, and Turkish Cypriots were the only Muslims eligible to move to Australia under the 'White Australia Policy' in the 1900s, so many Cypriots moved to those

---

[1] (The Guardian, 2010)

two countries under the threat of enosis, oppression and war.

By some calculations, there are now more Turkish Cypriot citizens living in the UK (approximately 130,000[1]) than there are native Turkish Cypriots living in Cyprus (approximately 88,000[2]). In fact, there are almost as many Cypriots living in just Haringey and Enfield alone (around 18,000[3]) as there are living in Kyrenia (20,851 as of 2011[4]).

There's a concern then, that with these particularly high levels of emigration, we might lose the unique Turkish Cypriot culture – a grave shame for Turkish Cypriots and their descendants around the world.

The Annan Plan

There have been international efforts to make the situation on the island fairer, most notably the Annan Plan in 2004 – a UN proposal, named after the UN Secretary General at the time Kofi Annan, intended to resolve the Cyprus dispute and reunify the island before the Republic of Cyprus accession to the EU. The

[1] (BBC, 2014)
[2] (UK Select Committee on Foreign Affairs, 2005)
[3] (BBC, 2005)
[4] (TRNC Census, 2011)

proposal suggested a restructuring of Cyprus, a new flag, and a new name – the United Cyprus Republic – which it described as "an independent state in the form of an indissoluble partnership, with a federal government and two equal constituent states, the Greek Cypriot State and the Turkish Cypriot State"[1]. The new country would be a federation of two states "of equal status"[2] joined together by a federal government apparatus. The central government would be made up of an equal number of Greek Cypriots and Turkish Cypriots, with a President and Vice President (one from each community) alternating in their functions every 20 months during five-year terms in office.

Cypriots would have citizenship of both their own federal state, as well as of Cyprus as a whole. Britain would keep their military bases, and the relationship with Turkey and Greece formed in the Treaty of Guarantee 1960 would still hold, and both sides would resolve that the "tragic events of the past shall never be repeated"[3], renouncing all violence and domination over one another. Each community would also make a

---

[1] (The United Nations, 2004, p. 7)
[2] (The United Nations, 2004, p. 18)
[3] (The United Nations, 2004, p. 6)

promise to respect "each other's cultural, religious, political, social and linguistic identity" [1].

The plan was put to an island-wide referendum in Cyprus in 2004. While it was overwhelmingly approved by the Turkish Cypriots with 64.9% voting to implement the plan, it was rejected overwhelmingly by 75.8% of Greek Cypriots. Turnout for the referendum was very high at 88% of Greek Cypriots and 87% of Turkish Cypriots[2], and so gives a very good idea of how each side saw the issue at the time.

Greek Cypriots voted against the plan for a number of reasons, but mainly seemed to cite irreconcilable differences around 1) Turkish settlers, and the Greek Cypriot desire for them to be expelled from the island, 2) the Republic of Cyprus not being able to recover as much land or property as they would like from the Turkish Cypriots, and 3) the Turkish Cypriot minority having too much political parity with the Greek Cypriot majority under the new plans.[3]

Following the referendum, the European Commission released a statement noting that it "deeply regrets that the Greek Cypriot community did not

---

[1] (The United Nations, 2004, p. 6)
[2] (UK Select Committee on Foreign Affairs, 2005)
[3] (Sözen, 2002, p. 19)

118

approve the comprehensive settlement of the Cyprus problem" and that they "would like to warmly congratulate Turkish Cypriots for their 'Yes' vote. This signals a clear desire of the community to resolve the island's problem. The Commission is ready to consider ways of further promoting economic development of the northern part of Cyprus"[1]. The Secretary General of the UN spoke of hopes "to eliminate unnecessary restrictions and barriers that have the effect of isolating the Turkish Cypriots and impeding their development"[2]. France, England, the US, Sweden, the Czech Republic, and many others made statements of regret that the Greek Cypriots could not find an agreement on the reunification of Cyprus, many also highlighting the injustice of the numerous embargoes on the Turkish Cypriots.[3]

Almost 20 years on, the international embargoes against the Turkish Republic of Northern Cyprus are still in place.

---

[1] (European Commission, 2004)
[2] (Republic of Turkey Ministry of Foreign Affairs, 2004)
[3] (Republic of Turkey Ministry of Foreign Affairs, 2004)

What next?

In 2006, a former Greek Cypriot MP claimed that the attempted coup of that year against Erdoğan in Turkey was a "lost opportunity" to reclaim the north by military force.[1] In 2020, a British peer in the House of Lords highlighted the struggle of the Turkish Cypriots, noting that "The north of the island continues to live under an unfair, unjust and unnecessary embargo", and calling on the British government to do something to help.[2] In 2004, the Greek Cypriot president at the time made outlandish claims that no Turkish Cypriots were killed at all between 1963 and 1974, denying that the massacres of 1963 and 1974 had ever even happened. In Paphos stands a life sized statue of EOKA and EOKA B military leader and terrorist Georgios Grivas with a reference to his apparent 'struggle' for 'liberation'.

Tensions are high amongst civilians too. Grafitti on each side of the green line, both positive and negative, is a common occurrence. Alongside the positive and hopeful messages, slogans like "death to Turks" have been seen scrawled across the walls of Nicosia.[3]

---

[1] (Cyprus Mail, 2016)
[2] (T-Vine, 2020)
[3] (Hurriyet, 2006)

Education is a problem too. A 2004 report by the Committee for Education Reform examined the Greek Cypriot educational system and found the education system to be "Greek-Cypriot centered, narrowly ethnocentric and culturally monolithic" and found it to be too "religious in character"[1]. In contrast, Turkish Cypriots are regarded as some of the "most secular Muslims in the world"[2] and their history school books have been found to, at least in part, aim for "the creation of empathy with Greek Cypriot suffering" [3]

Despite this hatred, Greek and Turkish Cypriots are one and the same. They share the same island, where members of both communities have lived, mostly in harmony, for centuries. Genetic analysis has even highlighted the similarities between the two communities, showing that they mainly share a common paternal ancestry from before even Ottoman times.[4] Their culture, their food, their music, and their history are intertwined with one another.

Hopefully, one day, the peaceful messages on the walls of Nicosia will drown out the aggressive ones, and Greek and Turkish Cypriot old friends will live together

---

[1] (Papadakis Y. , 2008, p. 11)
[2] (Yeşilada, 2009)
[3] (Papadakis Y. , 2008, p. 23)
[4] (Heraclides, et al., 2017)

121

in harmony once again. But for now, life carries on for Turkish-speaking and for Greek-speaking Cypriots, in the last physically divided capital city in the world.

BIBLIOGRAPHY

Özkul, P. E. (2020). *Social, Economic and Political History of Cyprus*. Retrieved from TRNC Public Information Office: https://pio.mfa.gov.ct.tr/en/social-economic-and-political-history-of-cyprus/

Özveren, E. (2012). The Geostrategic Importance of Cyprus: long term trends and prospects.

Al Jazeera. (2017, February 22). *Cyprus talks falter over nationalist commemoration row*. Retrieved November 2020, from Al Jazeera: https://www.aljazeera.com/news/2017/2/22/cyprus-talks-falter-over-nationalist-commemoration-row

American University. (1964). *U. S. Army Area Handbook for Cyprus*. Foreign Areas Studies, Washington D.C.

Baldwin, M. W., & Dickson, G. (2019, October). *Crusades*. Retrieved May 2020, from Encyclopædia Britannica: https://www.britannica.com/event/Crusades

Barchard, D. (2006). *The Fearless and Self-reliant Servant: The Life and Career of Sir Alfred Biliotti (1833–1915), An Italian Levantine in British Service.*

BBC. (2005). *Born Abroad: Cyprus*. Retrieved July 2020, from BBC News: http://news.bbc.co.uk/1/shared/spl/hi/uk/05/born_abroad/countries/html/cyprus.stm

BBC. (2014). *Turkish Today*. Retrieved July 2020, from BBC: http://www.bbc.co.uk/voices/multilingual/turkish.shtml

BBC News. (1999, November 20). *Clinton: US failed Greek democracy*. Retrieved May 2020, from BBC News: http://news.bbc.co.uk/1/hi/world/europe/529932.stm

Bicknell, P. J. (1977). Caesar, Antony, Cleopatra and Cyprus. *Latomus 36, 2.*

Bora, E. (2013). *Cyprus in International Law*. Ankara Bar Review.

Borowiec, A. (2000). *Cyprus: A Troubled Island.*

Brooks, S. T. (2006). *Byzantium, Faith, and Power (1261-1557): Perspectives on Late Byzantine Art and Culture.* New York: The Metropolitan Museum of Art.

Bryant, R., & Papadakis, Y. (2012). *Cyprus and the Politics of Memory: History, Community and Conflict.* I.B.Tauris.

Cagaptay, S. (2005). *Islam, Secularism and Nationalism in Modern Turkey: Who is a Turk?*

Cambazis, D. K. (2014, December 21). *http://www.havadiskibris.com/her-sey-buradan-basladi/*. Retrieved May 2020, from Havadis: http://www.havadiskibris.com/her-sey-buradan-basladi/

Campbell-Thomson, O. (2014). Pride and Prejudice: The Failure of UN Peace Brokering Efforts in Cyprus.

Cassia, P. S. (2005). *Bodies of Evidence: Burial, Memory and the Recovery of Missing Persons in Cyprus.* Berghahn Books.

Christiansen, A. (2005). *Crossing the Green Line: Anti-Settler Sentiment in Cyprus.* Macalester International.

Christofides, R. M. (2016). *'Are we turned Turks?': The Cyprus Problem in Othello, Soliman and Perseda, and Selimus.* Mediterranean Institute, University of Malta.

Chrysopoulos, P. (2018, March 3). Retrieved May 2020, from The Greek Reporter: https://greece.greekreporter.com/2018/03/03/grigoris-afxentiou-a-true-greek-cypriot-hero-video

Coşkun, Y. (2015). *The Cyprus Problem and Anglo-Turkish Relations 1967-1980.* University of East Anglia.

Commission of the European Communities. (2004). *Proposal for a COUNCIL REGULATION on special conditions for trade with those areas of the Republic of Cyprus in which the Government of the Republic of Cyprus does not exercise effective control.*

Cyprus Mail. (2016, July 18). *Attempted Turkish coup a 'lost opportunity' to reclaim north, says former MP.* Retrieved May 2020, from Cyprus Mail: https://cyprus-mail.com/2016/07/18/attempted-turkish-coup-lost-opportunity-reclaim-north-says-former-mp/

Cyprus Mail. (2020, November 10). *Thousands protest in north over Turkish interference.* Retrieved November 2020, from Cyprus Mail: https://cyprus-mail.com/2020/11/10/thousands-protest-in-north-over-turkish-interference/

Cyprus News Agency: News in English. (2010, 04 22). *Eu/cyprus : Nicosia Ready to Challenge Trnc Direct Trade Regulation.* Retrieved from http://www.hri.org/news/cyprus/cna/2010/10-04-22.cna.html

Davison, P. (2010, August 18). *Brigadier General Dimitrios Ioannidis: Soldier who served life imprisonment after leading coups in Greece and Cyprus.* Retrieved May 2020, from The Independent:

https://www.independent.co.uk/news/obituaries/brigadier-general-dimitrios-ioannidis-soldier-who-served-life-imprisonment-after-leading-coups-in-2055147.html

Demetriou, O. (2014). *'Struck by the Turks': reflections on Armenian refugeehood in Cyprus.*

Diez, T. (2001). *The European Union and the Cyprus Conflict: Modern Conflict, Postmodern Union.*

European Commission. (2004, April 26). *Commission statement following the outcome of the referendum in Cyprus.* Retrieved May 2020, from European Commission: https://ec.europa.eu/commission/presscorner/detail/en/IP_04_537

European Court of Human Rights. (2001). *Case of Cyprus v. Turkey Judgement.* Strasbourg.

European Parliament. (2019). *Tax crimes: special committee calls for a European financial police force.* Retrieved 2020, from https://www.europarl.europa.eu/news/en/press-room/20190225IPR28727/tax-crimes-special-committee-calls-for-a-european-financial-police-force

Finkel, C. (2012). Osman's Dream: The Story of the Ottoman Empire 1300-1923.

French, D. (2015). *Fighting EOKA: The British Counter-Insurgency Campaign on Cyprus, 1955-1959.* Oxford University Press.

Göktepe, C. (2005). The Cyprus Crisis of 1967 and its Effects on Turkey's Foreign Relations. *Middle Eastern Studies Vol. 41.*

Geopolitical Futures. (2020, May 1). Retrieved from https://geopoliticalfutures.com/cyprus-battle-east-west/

Gere, C. (2010). *Knossos and the Prophets of Modernism.* University of Chicago Press.

Gibbons, H. S. (1969). *Peace Without Honour.* ADA Publishing House.

Gjerstadt, E. (1979). The Phoenician colonization and expansion in Cyprus. *RDAC.*

Global IDP Project. (2005). *Profile of Internal Displacement: Cyprus.*

Goffman, D. (2002). *The Ottoman Empire and Early Modern Europe.* Cambridge University Press.

Halil, E. (2019, August 17). *Why the second phase of Turkey's Peace Operation in Cyprus was necessary.* Retrieved May 2020, from T-Vine: http://www.t-vine.com/why-the-second-phase-of-turkeys-peace-operation-in-cyprus-was-necessary/

Haralambous, C. H. (2017). *Making History (Disappear): Greece's Junta Trials and the Staging of Political Legitimation.* Johns Hopkins University Press.

Heraclides, A., Bashiardes, E., Fernández-Domínguez, E., Bertoncini, S., Chimonas, M., Christofi, V., . . . Wang, C.-C. (2017). *Y-chromosomal analysis of Greek Cypriots reveals a primarily common pre-Ottoman paternal ancestry with Turkish Cypriots.* PLOS ONE.

Hill, G. (2010). *A History of Cyprus, Volume 4.* Cambridge University Press.

Hirschfeld, N. (2010). Cyprus. In M. Gagarin. *The Oxford Encyclopedia of Ancient Greece and Rome.*

Hoffmeister, F. (2006). *Legal Aspects of the Cyprus Problem: Annan Plan and EU Accession.*

Holland, R. (1998). *Britain and the Revolt in Cyprus, 1954-1959.* Clarendon Press.

Holland, R. F. (1994). *Emergencies and Disorder in the European Empires After 1945.* Routledge.

Horgan, J., & Braddock, K. (2012). *Terrorism Studies.* London: Routledge.

Hurriyet. (2006, December 27). *Racist slogans on Nicosian buildings raise tensions in Cyprus.* Retrieved May 2020, from https://www.hurriyet.com.tr/gundem/racist-slogans-on-nicosian-buildings-raise-tensions-in-cyprus-5683061

Kadioğlu, P. (2010). *The rise of ethno-nationalism in Cyprus under the British rule: 1878-1960.* MIDDLE EAST TECHNICAL UNIVERSITY.

Karyos, A. (2009). EOKA and Enosis in 1955-59: Motive and Aspiration Reconsidered.

Ker-Lindsay, J. (2009, April). *Britain and the Cyprus Crisis 1963-1964.*

Ker-Lindsay, J. (2017). *Great powers, counter secession and nonrecognition: Britain and the 1983 unilateral declaration of independence of the "Turkish Republic of Northern Cyprus".*

Kiralp, S. (2014). *National identity and elite interests: Makarios and Greek Cypriot nationalism (1967-1974).* Keele University.

Kovras, I. (2014). *Truth Recovery and Transitional Justice: Deferring human rights issues.* Routledge.

Lieberman, B. (2013). *Terrible Fate: Ethnic Cleansing in the Making of Modern Europe.* Rowman & Littlefield.

Lynch, R. J. (2016). Cyprus and Its Legal and Historiographical Significance in Early Islamic History. *Journal of the American Oriental Society 136*.

M.Ellis, W. (1994). *Ptolemy of Egypt.*

Makarios. (1974, July 19). Retrieved May 2020, from http://www.cypnet.co.uk/ncyprus/history/republic/makarios-speech.html#speech

Mark, J. J. (2014, June 30). *Neo-Assyrian Empire.* Retrieved May 2020, from Ancient History Encyclopedia: https://www.ancient.eu/Neo-Assyrian_Empire/

Melson, M. M. (2010). *Trade and exchange in the Neolithic Near East: Implications of obsidian remains from Ais Yiorkis, Cyprus.* UNLV.

Menache, S. (2003). *Clement V.* University of Haifa, Israel.

Merriam-Webster Inc. (2020, January 28). *The Merriam-Webster.com Dictionary.* Retrieved from https://www.merriam-webster.com/dictionary/copper

Ministry of Foreign Affairs, Republic of Cyprus. (1960, August 16). *No.5475. Treaty of Guarantee.* Retrieved May 2020, from https://www.mfa.gr/images/docs/kypriako/treaty_of_guarantee.pdf

Mirbagheri, F. (1998). *Cyprus and International Peacemaking 1964-1986.* Routledge.

Newman, P. (1940). *A Short History of Cyprus.* London: Longmans, Green & Co.

Newsinger, J. (2015). *British Counterinsurgency.* Palgrave Macmillan.

Novo, A. R. (2015). An Insoluble Problem: The Harding-Makarios Negotiations, Turkey, and the Cause of Cypriot Enosis. *The National Defence University Journal of Mediterranean Studies.*

Oberling, P. (1982). *The road to Bellapais: the Turkish Cypriot exodus to northern Cyprus.* Social Science Monographs.

Papacostas, T. (2001). *The Economy of Late Antique Cyprus. In: Economy and Exchange in the East Mediterranean during Late Antiquity.* Oxford: Oxbow Books.

Papadakis, Y. (2005). *Locating the Cyprus Problem: Ethnic Conflict and the Politics of Space.* University of Cyprus.

Papadakis, Y. (2008). *History Education in Divided Cyprus: A Comparison of Greek Cypriot and Turkish Cypriot Schoolbooks on the "History of Cyprus".* PRIO Cyprus Centre.

Papaeti, A. (2013). *Music, Torture, Testimony: Reopening the Case of the Greek Junta (1967–1974).*

Parker, S. T. (1976). The Objectives and Strategy of Cimon's Expedition to Cyprus. *The American Journal of Philology, 97.*

Pegg, S. (1998). *International Society and the de Facto State.* Ashgate Publishing.

Politico. (2019). *Turkish Cypriots fear being part of Erdoğan's 'pious generation'.* Retrieved July 2020, from Politico.eu: https://www.politico.eu/article/turkish-cypriots-fear-recep-tayyip-erdogan-pious-generation-islam-mosque/

Rapoport, D. (2013). The four waves of modern terror: International dimensions and consequences. *An International History of Terrorism: Western and Non-Western Experiences.*

Republic of Turkey Ministry of Foreign Affairs. (2004). *What the World said After the Referanda.* Retrieved May 2020, from Republic of Turkey Ministry of Foreign Affairs: http://www.mfa.gov.tr/what-the-world-said-after-the-referanda.en.mfa

Richmond, O. P., & Ker-Lindsay, J. (2001). *The Work of the UN in Cyprus: Promoting Peace and Development.* Palgrave Macmillan.

Richter, H. (2006). *Geschichte der Insel Zypern.* Harrassowitz.

Richter, H. (2011). *History of Cyprus: Volume 2.* Harrassowitz.

Sözen, A. (2002). *The Fall and the Rise of the Consociational Democracy in Cyprus.* Istanbul: University of Bahcesehir.

Safty, A. (2011). *The Cyprus Question: Diplomacy and International Law.*

Safty, D. A. (2011). *The Cyprus Question: Diplomacy and International Law .*

Smilden, J.-E. (2007). When the Turks saved the Greek Cypriots: Selective Memories of 300 years under Ottoman Rule.

Solsten, E. (1991). *Cyprus: A Country Study.* Washington, D.C.: Library of Congress. Federal Research Division.

Tahsin, A. H. (2001). *He Anodos Tou: Denktas Sten Koryphe.* Ekdoseis Diaphaneia.

The Guardian. (1999, July 17). *Split for infinity?* Retrieved May 2020, from https://www.theguardian.com/theguardian/1999/jul/17/weekend7.weekend

The Guardian. (2010, July 9). *Jennifer Lopez cancels northern Cyprus gig.* Retrieved May 2020, from The Guardian: https://www.theguardian.com/world/2010/jul/09/jennifer-lopez-cancels-cyprus-gig

The Guardian. (2020). *Turkish Cypriot leader warns Cyprus is facing permanent partition.* Retrieved July 2020, from The Guardian: https://www.theguardian.com/world/2020/feb/06/turkish-cypriot-leader-warns-cyprus-facing-permanent-partition-mustafa-akinci

The National. (2020, May 1). Retrieved from https://www.thenational.ae/world/greek-cyprus-plays-role-in-fight-against-isil-1.653740

The Telegraph. (2010, August 17). *Obituaries: Dimitrios Ioannidis.* Retrieved May 2020, from https://www.telegraph.co.uk/news/obituaries/military-obituaries/7950781/Dimitrios-Ioannidis.html

The United Nations. (2004, March 31). *The Comprehensive Settlement of the Cyprus Problem.*

The United Nations. (2020, May 20). *1967 Crisis.* Retrieved May 2020, from UN Missions: https://unficyp.unmissions.org/1967-crisis

TRNC Census. (2011). *KKTC NÜFUS SAYIMI.*

TRNC Ministry of Foreign Affairs. (2020). *Historical Background.* Retrieved July 2020, from TRNC Government Website: https://mfa.gov.ct.tr/cyprus-negotiation-process/historical-background

T-Vine. (2020, January 15). *Lord Sharkey calls on British government to end international isolation of Turkish Cypriots.* Retrieved May 2020, from T-Vine: http://www.t-vine.com/lord-sharkey-calls-on-british-government-to-end-international-isolation-of-turkish-cypriots/

UK Select Committee on Foreign Affairs. (2004). *Written evidence submitted by the Turkish Republic of Northern Cyprus, President's Office.* Retrieved July 2020, from UK Parliament: https://publications.parliament.uk/pa/cm200405/cmselect/cmfaff/113/113we23.htm

UK Select Committee on Foreign Affairs. (2005, February 22). Retrieved May 2020, from UK Parliament Publications: https://publications.parliament.uk/pa/cm200405/cmselect/cmfaff/113/11305.htm

UK Select Committee on Foreign Affairs. (2005). *HOW MANY TURKISH CYPRIOTS REMAIN IN CYPRUS.* Retrieved July 2020, from UK Parliament: https://publications.parliament.uk/pa/cm200405/cmselect/cmfaff/113/113we33.htm

UN Security Council. (1964, September 10). Retrieved May 2020, from Security Council Report: https://www.securitycouncilreport.org/atf/cf/%7B65BFCF9B-

6D27-4E9C-8CD3-
CF6E4FF96FF9%7D/Cyprus%20S%205950.pdf

UN Security Council. (1975). *Resolution 367.*

UN Security Council Resolution 541 and 550. (1983, 1984).
Retrieved from http://unscr.com/en/resolutions

United States. Congress. Senate. Committee on the
Judiciary. Subcommittee to Investigate Problems Connected
with Refugees and Escapees. (1974). *Humanitarian Problems on
Cyprus: Hearing Before the Subcommittee to Investigate Problems
Connected with Refugees and Escapees of the Committee on the
Judiciary, United States Senate, Ninety-third Congress, Second
Session, Part 1.* U.S. Government Printing Office.

Varnava, A. (2010). Reinterpreting Macmillan's Cyprus
policy, 1957–1960. *Cyprus Review.*

Vigne, J.-D., Guilaine, J., Debue, K., & Haye. (2004). *Early
Taming of the Cat in Cyprus.* New York, NY: Science.

World Bank. (2020). Retrieved 2020, from
https://datahelpdesk.worldbank.org/knowledgebase/articles/9
06519#High_income

Yeşilada, B. (2009). Islam and the Turkish Cypriots. *SAGE
Journals.*

Yosef, K. (2013). *The term mamluk and slave status during
the Mamluk Sultanate.* Bar Ilan University, Israel.

Zavagno, L. (2013). Two hegemonies, one island: Cyprus as
a "Middle Ground" between the Byzantines and the Arabs (650-
850 A.D.).

Printed in Great Britain
by Amazon

54445399R00083